AWAKENING THE SPIRIT

INSPIRING THE SOUL

AWAKENING THE SPIRIT,
INSPIRING THE SOUL

30 STORIES
of
INTERSPIRITUAL DISCOVERY
in the Community of Faiths

Edited by
Brother Wayne Teasdale
and **Martha Howard,** MD

Foreword by
Joan Borysenko, PhD

Walking Together, Finding the Way
SKYLIGHT PATHS® Publishing
NASHVILLE, TENNESSEE

Awakening the Spirit, Inspiring the Soul:
30 Stories of Interspiritual Discovery in the Community of Faiths

Library of Congress Cataloging-in-Publication Data
Awakening the spirit, inspiring the soul : 30 stories of interspiritual discovery in the community of faiths / edited by Wayne Teasdale and Martha Howard; foreword by Joan Borysenko.
       p. cm.
ISBN 1-59473-039-3 (hardcover)
1. Spiritual life. I. Teasdale, Wayne. II. Howard, Martha.
BL624.A93 2004
204'.4'0922—dc22   2004004156

10 9 8 7 6 5 4 3 2

Manufactured in the United States of America

SkyLight Paths is creating a place where people of different spiritual traditions come together for challenge and inspiration, a place where we can help each other understand the mystery that lies at the heart of our existence.

SkyLight Paths sees both believers and seekers as a community that increasingly transcends traditional boundaries of religion and denomination—people wanting to learn from each other, walking together, finding the way.

Cover design: Sara Dismukes
Cover art: *A Sabbath for the Land* (© 2003) was painted by Michael Bogdanow (http://www.MichaelBogdanow.com). It was inspired by and includes Hebrew text from the Torah portion *Behar*, Leviticus XXV–XXVI, which addresses the rule of leaving the land fallow every seven years, plus a "Jubilee" year every forty-nine years. The painting and reproductions of it are part of the artist's *Visions of Torah* series of contemporary, spiritual paintings and reproduc-tions inspired by Judaic texts.

SkyLight Paths, "Walking Together, Finding the Way" and colophon are trademarks of LongHill Partners, Inc., registered in the U.S. Patent and Trademark Office.

Walking Together, Finding the Way

Published by SkyLight Paths Publishing
A Division of LongHill Partners, Inc.
An Imprint of Turner Publishing Company
4507 Charlotte Avenue, Suite 100
Nashville, TN 37209

Tel: (615) 255-2665
www.skylightpaths.com

Contents

Foreword

JOAN BORYSENKO, PhD

NEARLY THIRTY YEARS AGO, when my sons Justin and Andrei were little guys, we sat together one night reading a bedtime story from the New Testament. Earlier in the evening our family had gone to Sufi dancing hosted by a nearby Episcopal seminary. The following week we would start preparations for the Jewish Passover. My husband and I were also deeply involved with Paramahansa Yogananda's Self-Realization Fellowship, studying points of unity between yoga philosophy and Christianity in our search for the Divine Beloved.

Sound odd? The kind of interreligious study and practice that my children grew up with had its beginnings as a grass-roots movement among the baby boomers three decades back. Wade Clark Roof, a professor of religion at the University of California, Santa Barbara, identified this trend in his 1993 best seller, *A Generation of Seekers: The Spiritual Lives of the Baby Boom Generation*. He's continued to follow the baby boomers and ask questions about the kind of practical, engaged spirituality so many of them continue to seek.

I've been intrigued by a related question concerning the spiritual lives of the baby boomer's children. How do kids like Justin and Andrei, raised in an interreligious environment, find a path that can go the distance and take them home? Will the eclectic spirituality with which they were raised do its job both as a moral compass and as a psychospiritual guide that can help them see and dismantle the false self and live instead from Divine Essence? As the old adage warns, are we raising a generation to dig a hundred shallow wells rather than one deep well that will yield living waters for the benefit of the larger human family?

When my boys were young men of twenty and sixteen, we sat together at the kitchen table one morning, reflecting on their interfaith upbringing. "Do you consider yourselves part of any particular religion?" I asked. They looked at me incredulously and blurted out, almost in unison, "We're Jews, of course."

Judaism is my religion of origin, and by Jewish law a mother's children are automatically members of the faith. The celebration of holy days with grandparents, aunts, uncles, and cousins was a deep bond to Judaism for the boys, even though they hadn't been sent to Hebrew school. As a young man, Justin was angry about the loss of a traditional Jewish education. He felt deprived of his heritage and wanted to become a bar mitzvah some day. His brother, Andrei, in contrast, expressed relief that he'd been spared what he thought of as "early programming." He argued that being exposed to different religions and growth philosophies as a child would allow him to find his own authentic path as an adult. He might or might not choose to be a bar mitzvah some day, but at least the choice would be his.

If I had the opportunity to raise my precious boys again, I would have looked for a liberal Jewish congregation and grounded them firmly in their root tradition while simultaneously exposing them to the interreligious experience. As young men, neither of them is deeply committed to any spiritual path. But this is far from unusual at their ages. As I've listened to people's spiritual autobiographies over the years, the conversion experiences that call us home to the Divine Beloved often come later in life, frequently in the throes of a dark night of the soul that shatters the known world and delivers us to the mysterious unknown, where our soul can more easily hear the divine voice calling.

Many of the fascinating spiritual autobiographies collected in this volume are those of young people like my sons. They are not just Americans, or children of baby boomers. These young voices come from many cultures and religious traditions. A common thread in most of these stories is that the writers heard the "call" when they were children. The development of their good hearts had been supported by parents who practiced what they preached. The religious tradition they were affiliated with mattered far less than the example of a loving, caring life.

The process of writing spiritual autobiography is a profound exercise, often filled with fresh revelation. The process is deepened even further when the member of a group of friends, family members, or fellow travelers each write an autobiography to share with the rest of the group. Fifteen years ago I was part of an ecumenical women's circle. The writing and sharing of spiritual autobiography occupied our first several sessions. The experience was so intimate, authentic, and real that we bonded instantly from our hearts. The field of love, kindness and authenticity that resulted set the tone for years of friendship, spiritual practice, and mutual growth.

There is a thirst for authentic connection in our scattered, busy, speedy culture. Sharing deeply from the soul and being received with an open heart satisfies that thirst. Being seen and acknowledged cultivates the soil of our good hearts. In the back of this book you'll find a space to write your spiritual autobiography. My hope is that you'll share it with others and hear their stories in turn. May the heartfelt conversation that results be a deep inquiry for you all into the meaning of being both fully human and fully divine. That is what this beautiful book, and the integral spirituality it addresses so elegantly, is all about.

Introduction

ALL OF THE CONTRIBUTORS to this book have made intensely personal searches for higher meaning in their lives, and most of them began very young. Their religious and spiritual experiences as children and young people might well be required reading for all parents, religious leaders, and teachers. They are a testimonial to the idea that teaching is done almost exclusively by example, not with words. Gaps between preaching and practice more often than not cause rejection of what we are preaching. Several writers emphasize the importance of teachers and mentors as models for inspiring us to seek lives of practical spirituality. These teachers are all distinguished by their ability to serve as living illustrations of their beliefs.

These extraordinary stories are spiritual autobiographies that reveal an essential need for the human spirit: the existence of many paths to the experience and the manifestation of the Divine. The writers come from different faiths, ages, and backgrounds. Their accounts of life-changing spiritual events and realizations are remarkable for their individuality; yet all have common threads.

In the stories, the search for true integration of the life of the spirit into daily life unfailingly draws our writers into remarkable transformations: sometimes in their original faith, and sometimes in a different one, an interfaith practice, or a practice of ethics that does not necessarily involve any formal religion.

What is it about these stories that can benefit us? Why is it important to read them and to generate our own stories? Kindness, and all of the good qualities of which we are capable as human beings, are worth cultivating. These stories are practical revelations of the kinds of responses and actions in daily life that develop the skills and focus to make kindness, understanding, mutual respect, generosity, honesty, patience, wisdom, and the golden rule a daily reality. They show how ordinary people just like ourselves arrive at the kind of mental and emotional stability produced by stillness (whether we call it prayer, meditation, or something else) and bring forth the highest potential of their own minds and hearts.

In one story, encountering sincere practitioners of two different faiths brings a young seeker back to his Islamic roots. At first, the writer lives in a Catholic Worker house. He sees people supported and treated kindly when they need it most. Then he goes to visit his Islamic grandmother in India. He discovers that she lives her faith by housing and supporting, in her own home, women who have been victims of domestic violence and abuse. There is his own grandmother, in the context of a completely different country and faith, essentially doing the same thing that he has just seen in the Catholic Worker house. This makes the connection that brings him back to Islam and into the interfaith movement.

If we are to respond differently in our lives, we must know how we get triggered off into reactions of anger or irritation or revenge, how to process these reactions, and to choose to respond with something that makes the situation better, rather than worse. It is important to hear, in these stories, how someone else has approached this challenging task. One of the stories illustrates the importance of "friendly ground" and of dialogue in this process. A young woman from the University of Chicago finds herself in South Africa, in the same small group with a young Islamic man from the same university. Back at home, they have been on opposite sides of a campus battle of gigantic religious and political proportions. In the atmosphere of the Parliament of the World's Religions and activities in South Africa, things begin to change.

We all know what goodness is and what good human qualities are. We would all really rather live in a loving, cooperative atmosphere. Somehow, we have not yet believed that this is possible. Too often we have allowed ourselves to be carried away by our worst tendencies. Yet, in the stories we see a Catholic priest coming to terms with the fact that he was a Jewish "hidden child" of the Holocaust, and another Holocaust survivor coming, later in life, to forgive his Nazi captors. A young man from Soweto turns from suspicion to trust and friendship in the process of working with a peace organization and living in a home with white people. Each individual's experience is revealed in its unique qualities and in its value.

It is a priority now to support ourselves, and one another, in living up to the best of our good human qualities, whether or not we practice a religion. The signals of a new age of spiritual understanding and practice are present in these stories. The value of each person's contribution to a larger transformation is immeasurable. In this spirit, we invite you to discover, live, write, and share the stories of your own transformations. The blank journal pages at the end of this book are a place to begin.

The Golden Rule: An Evolutionary Future

W E HAVE EXTRAORDINARY CHOICES at this time: we can bring about our own mass extinction, we can devolve into global warlordism, or we can evolve and become a different type of being on the earth. A deliberate and conscious change is called for, toward the recognition of all beings as belonging to the same "body as a whole." We could benefit by the realization that to harm another being, another part of this same body, is like chopping off our own hand or foot.

The nature of survival has changed, almost in an instant. The Darwinian "survival of the fittest" (meaning species with the greatest ability to adapt physically, for the moment, to the demands of the environment) is no longer working. That type of survival has brought about the temporary "rule" of a type of organism on the earth; at present, we appear to be the rulers.

As human beings we have the instincts, generally, to love and nurture our own and to protect ourselves against those we perceive to be a threat. But "flight or fight" is no longer adaptive. Some of the same traits that may have contributed to survival, in the Darwinian sense, at an earlier time in our evolution, now may well contain the seeds of our destruction.

Past sources of evolutionary change have been material. Now could be the time for an evolution of consciousness, led by a global effort to think, speak, and act in ways that support the understanding of ourselves as a great being. What if we really did practice the Golden Rule? What if we had relationships with everyone on earth that were like those we have with our nearest and dearest family members and friends?

How do we make this evolutionary change? We are just beginning to understand some of the ways to proceed at this time. The Golden Rule is a common thread and a good place to start.

THE GOLDEN RULES OF WORLD RELIGIONS

These are the Golden Rules of many of the world religions, gathered for the Golden Rule poster by Paul McKenna and presented to Mrs. Gillian Sorensen, Assistant Secretary General of the United Nations, on January 4, 2002.

Aboriginal Spirituality

We are as much alive as we keep the Earth alive.

—Chief Dan George

Baha'i

Lay not on any soul a load that you would not wish to be laid upon you, and desire not for anyone the things you would not desire for yourself.

—Baha'u'llah, Gleanings

Buddhism

Treat not others in ways that you yourself would find hurtful.

—The Buddha, Udana-Varga 5.18

Christianity

In everything, do to others as you would have them do to you; for this is the law and the prophets.

—Jesus, Matthew 7:12

Confucianism

One word which sums up the basis of all good conduct … loving-kindness. Do not do to others what you do not want done to yourself.

—Confucius, Analects 15.23

Hinduism

This is the sum of duty: do not do to others what would cause pain if done to you.

—Mahabharata 5:1517

Islam

Not one of you truly believes until you wish for others what you wish for yourself.

—Fourth Hadith of an-Nawawi 13

Jainism

One should treat all creatures in the world as one would like to be treated.

—Mahavira, Sutrakritanga

Judaism

What is hateful to you, do not do to your neighbor. This is the whole Torah; all the rest is commentary.

—Hillel, Talmud, Shabbath 31a

Shinto

The heart of the person before you is a mirror. See there your own form.

Sikhism

I am a stranger to no one; and no one is a stranger to me. Indeed, I am a friend to all.

—Guru Granth Sahib, p. 1299

Sufism

The basis of Sufism is consideration of the hearts and feelings of others. If you haven't the will to gladden someone's heart, then at least beware lest you hurt someone's heart for on our path, no sin exists but this.

—Dr. Javad Nurbakhsh, Master of the Nimatullahi Sufi Order

Taoism

Regard your neighbor's gain as your own gain and your neighbor's loss as your own loss.

—T'ai Shang Kan Ying P'ien, 213–218

Unitarianism

We affirm and promote respect for the interdependent web of all existence, of which we are a part.

—Unitarian principle

Wicca

An it harm no one, do what thou wilt (i.e., do what you wish, as long as it harms nobody, including yourself.)

—The Wiccan Rede

Yoruba

One going to take a pointed stick to pinch a baby bird should first try it on himself to feel how it hurts.

Zoroastrianism

Do not do unto others whatever is injurious to yourself.

—Shayast-na-Shayast 13.29

GOLDEN RULES FOR A CULTURE OF PEACE

This statement was made at the presentation of the Golden Rule poster at the United Nations.

Because the United Nations is a home for our highest human ideals, and because the world's religions have a duty to articulate and promote those ideals, we are honored to present you with "The Golden Rule." In this poster, thirteen religious and spiritual traditions state a universal principle in elegant and distinctive forms. These Golden Rules are evidence of a Global Ethic that transcends nations, civilizations, and religions. Yet no other statements so clearly summarize the simple practices of kindness and sustainable human conduct. In recent years, gatherings of religious and spiritual leaders have confirmed that "this ancient precept is found and has persisted in many religious and ethical traditions of humankind for thousands of years … [and] should be the irrevocable, unconditional norm for all areas of life, for families and communities, for races, nations, and religions" (*Toward a Global Ethic*). The United Nations provides a unique forum where the subtleties of this universal principle can be translated into the realm of international affairs. We are inspired by key United Nations documents such as the Universal Declaration of Human Rights and its premise that those rights we wish for ourselves shall be granted to others as well. Equally challenging is the principle that no nation will find peace until it wants for others the same peace and security it seeks for itself. We believe that these Golden

Rules, also known as the "law of reciprocity," must be obeyed by all nations, and that, in the interests of global security, no nations or leaders may exempt themselves. Whatever is hateful or injurious to ourselves, we must not do to others. Failure to adhere to these moral principles brings great hazards to all, ranging from unsustainable development practices to environmental crises and nuclear threats with their inherent potential for catastrophe. Nations must treat other nations as they wish to be treated. Together, these precepts remind us that our diversity can flourish within a greater and simpler unity—the human family, with its common origins, needs, and aspirations. The Golden Rules teach that no one—no nation, culture, or religion—is an island unto itself. Drawing on time-tested wisdom and experience, they presume our interdependence and declare our personal responsibility for the common good.

Look Inside, Look Outside: Concentric Circles of Interfaith Action

ABRA POLLACK

T HE FIRST OPEN CONVERSATION about religion that I had with a Muslim took place in another country, on the other side of the world, with a young man who lived in a dorm five blocks from mine in Chicago. The idea of dialogue appealed to me because, under the circumstances, it served as a vehicle for forming an unlikely friendship. Now, as a college junior who has helped organize interfaith programming on campus and in the city of Chicago, I understand interfaith exchange to be effective at a microcosmic level in building interpersonal relationships, as well as at a macrocosmic level of transforming communities. As a result of this development, which began on my University of Chicago delegation to South Africa, interfaith exchange has empowered me to be a more reflective Jew, as well as a more versatile citizen who feels comfortable taking on the problems of our multifaith, multifaceted society.

My initial encounter with interfaith dialogue arose as a reaction to finding myself touring South Africa in a group of people possessing an intimidating level of diversity. The delegation's focus on human rights had attracted graduate and undergraduate students who were diverse

1

in color, age, religion, nationality, academic expertise, and political loyalty. In particular, I noticed Tala and Mohanad, both of Palestinian background. I was afraid to speak to them, worried that my casual banter about the length of our bus rides or even a more profound observation on South African apartheid might seem hollow in light of the larger question that seemed to permeate my mind like an atmosphere, refusing to dissipate or relent.

I had spent the previous year heavily involved in activism on behalf of Israel. Many other campus groups, including the Muslim Students' Association and the Arab Union, took diametrically opposing stances to my pro-Israel group and to what they perceived to be the official viewpoint of Hillel, the Jewish students' center. Certain members of the Arab and Muslim groups believed that all Jewish students were pro-Israel and thus were likely to be involved in activities that were an anathema to their understanding of Israel as an unjust occupier. The chasm between our communities widened as flyers from both sides were repeatedly vandalized and as protests on the quads were met with counterdemonstrations. This was the complex matter I faced while spending two emotionally and intellectually intense weeks learning about South Africa's history of injustice and human rights abuses and, inevitably, noticing parallels with the Palestinian-Israeli conflict. For me, and for Tala and Mohanad, this was the elephant in the room.

I made my first deliberate effort to speak to Mohanad during our group's visit to the South-End Museum. The museum's mission is to preserve the history of the South-End neighborhood, where, in previous decades, multiple ethnic and religious groups had coexisted peacefully. The neighborhood's multiculturalism had been obliterated with the implementation of the Group Areas Act of 1950, which forced colored (mixed-race) South Africans to relocate in alternative, less desirable areas of real estate. While our group shuffled through the exhibits, I sidled up next to Mohanad and asked him, "What do you think?" The question was innocuous enough to elicit an equally innocent response, but Mohanad took it as his cue to open up, and he responded with the full weight of his troubled conscience. Listening to him speak, I felt relieved to have established a small space of honesty and calm between us.

Mohanad and I continued to dialogue over the next few days and indeed for the rest of the trip. We sat next to each other during bus rides, and at times, our political discussions and reflections on South Africa turned into angry debates. But what also emerged from our conversations, independent of my original intentions, was an ongoing dialogue about Islam and Judaism. We noted the linguistic similarities between our religions' holy languages, Hebrew and Arabic. Mohanad was my guide in my first-ever visit to a mosque, at a historical site in Port Elizabeth. Rosh Hashanah fell during our trip, and Mohanad and I made plans for him to attend services with me. He would have come, too, if he hadn't been late getting dressed and hadn't missed the taxi that took us to the synagogue.

One particularly poignant memory from the delegation is of an afternoon when our group took a short detour to a nearby ranch that offered horseback riding. After Mohanad and I had finished the trail, we wandered over to sit at some picnic tables and relax. It was at this setting that Mohanad inquired about Jewish liturgy: the various prayers it encompasses, the parallels between Hebrew and Islamic prayer vocabulary. He asked me to demonstrate. This is the one time in my life that I have chanted the *V'ahavta* (devotion to God) while sitting on a picnic bench at a ranch in South Africa. It seemed out of place, but somehow intimate and worthwhile, to share the *V'ahavta* at that specific time and place, and with Mohanad.

At the microcosmic level, the benefits of my dialogue with Mohanad were clear. The dialogue had afforded me a glimpse of the striking similarities between our two Abrahamic faiths. But our dialogue also enabled me to form a bittersweet friendship that was unlike most of my previous relationships involving individuals of different backgrounds. While growing up in suburban New Jersey, I often felt that despite the American rhetoric of celebrating differences, the easiest way to fit into the mainstream was to simply not talk about whatever made someone culturally different—such as my Judaism, which has situated me in the minority throughout my academic career. My friendship with Mohanad was distinctive because from its inception, we included an acknowledgment of our religious and political backgrounds into our conversations—and, in fact, many of our conversations centered on these differences. As a result, I felt supported and safe around him, comfortable in the understanding that he cared enough about my identity to ask the tough questions, and not just let my Jewishness fade into the background. Similarly, Mohanad felt comfortable opening up to me about religious issues, such as his concern over whether our group's meals were *halal* (prepared according to the Muslim dietary code) and his reaction to finding out that historically, South Africa's (primarily South Asian) Muslims had served as the nation's slave class.

At the microcosmic level, interfaith exchange promotes interpersonal relationships based on mutual recognition of religious identities. But affirming the religious identity of the "Other" can also be extremely beneficial on a macrocosmic level. One example would be the tensions that American society has faced in protecting Muslim and Jewish communities from incitements to hatred, which, in recent times, have threatened religious communities across the globe, including in the United States. When leaders of institutions such as universities, cities, or even nations are outspoken in recognizing and reaching out to the diverse religious groups of their constituency, such statements can serve as a deterrent to intolerance by encouraging people to acknowledge their questions and fears. In this way, interfaith exchange can redirect an interpersonal, local, or national atmosphere from one of silent or vocal antagonism to one of humble inclusiveness.

At the University of Chicago, I have worked for the past year with the help of Mohanad, as well as several other key students, to create interfaith opportunities that can build inclusiveness from the interpersonal level all the way to the broader campus community. In November 2002, Mohanad and I helped coordinate an interfaith *iftar* (break-the-fast) during Ramadan for students from Hillel, the Muslim Students Association, and Brent House, the campus Episcopalian ministry. Although Mohanad has now graduated, the interfaith *iftar* took place once again this year.

Our campus newspaper, *The Maroon*, covered the event both years, and it publicized the event as a refreshing alternative to the more frequent news reports of interreligious violence. In addition, two other students, Ira and Javeria, used the November 2002 *iftar* as a venue to announce their plans to launch a Jewish-Muslim dialogue group (JMD) and to invite members of the religious communities present to take part in the dialogue. The JMD has met on a weekly basis throughout the school year since its formation in January 2003. This fall, in my capacity as Hillel Commemorations Chair, a fellow Hillel board member and I put together an observance of the *Kristallnacht* ("Night of the broken glass") anniversary. We focused on combating hate crimes, and we included representatives from communities of several different faiths.

In elementary school, my mother would visit my class each year around Hanukkah and Passover bringing stories and religious implements with her to educate young minds about Jewish traditions. While I loved having my mother—and my tradition—at the center of attention, it felt strange to have Judaism so revealed, so prominent, when I was used to getting away with not having to explain the intimate details of why I was different. Now, in my third year of college, I realize that the warm feeling of opening up about one's religious identity does not have to be restricted to a twice-a-year occurrence. My experiences have taught me that interfaith exchange, on both the microcosmic and macrocosmic levels, can empower communities and can counterbalance the hostility that results from an environment of silence and suspicion. Achieving religious inclusiveness and working to override intolerance can seem to be a daunting task, no matter what size the community may be. Yet, my intuition is that interfaith action is a powerful social mechanism that is accessible and full of potential, a tool that we must put to use, no matter how disjointed and aloof the world around us may seem. As it says in Chapter 3 of *Pirkei Avot* ("Teachings of the Fathers," a celebrated Jewish text of ethical insights):

The day is short, and the work is hard, but though it is not your job to finish the work, neither are you free to desist from it.

Know Love, Know Life

SHIRLEY BAAS

L ISTEN TO WHAT I have to tell you as an African.
I was born on the first of December, 1984, in a family of three
brothers and two sisters. I lived all my life in Dobsonville, Soweto,
where people were separated by the languages they spoke. Discrimina-
tion and hatred was all over, and children suffered most.

I never knew the horror of what could pour out of the human heart,
the horror of what seemed most demented because the main perpetra-
tors of it were children and children learnt it from their parents, but
children went a little further.

No love, no life. Know love, know life. I know that life is full of cactus,
but we don't have to sit on it. Children absorb everything that comes their
way, and it is hard to fix things at a later stage. I always wished to do something to change that but felt I did not have time. Actually it was that famous
excuse: "Because it does not happen to me, it does not affect me."

After finishing matric in 2002 I wasn't financially able to further
my studies, so I went ahead and joined Play for Peace. I gave my time
with passion to these children, and I live in compassion with them.
This counts as one of my major changes in my life. If only people knew
that you can choose to live your life in PEACE or you can choose to live
your life in pieces, your life will be PEACEFUL when you give up your
right to be right for your right to be happy.

Down from the Mountain

APRIL KUNZE

A T A SUMMER CAMP just outside of Almaty, the capital of Kazakhstan, a belligerent sixteen-year-old boy disrupted my beginning English class with an uprising against me. In street-worn Russian, he rose to a battle of worldviews, ethics and cultural integrity: "The biggest sin in *my* religion is for me to convert to another religion. I am here to learn English, not to become a Christian." Burkut, a more rebellious than devout Muslim, and most of his friends at "English Camp" had figured out that the teachers' use of the New Testament in the Bible as a study text was attached to another agenda that had little to do with English as a second language. I was eighteen, and this was my second overseas evangelism trip. The summer before, I had spent six weeks hiking among villages on the slopes of Mt. Kilimanjaro in Tanzania: showing the Jesus film, preaching through puppet shows, and holding church services for those who might be saved.

From the time when I began to search for an articulation of my highest purpose in life, it has involved two elements: union with God and being a positive force in the world. I considered the latter an essential byproduct of the first and saw the real value of my Christianity within this relationship. The Christian mentors that helped to shape my faith journey always lived out a faith that was governed by the biblical teaching "Faith without works is dead" (James 2:26).

My mom, a hyper-practical and extremely generous Minnesota Lutheran, has always entertained dreams of unlimited love and enlightened hospitality. At eighteen she formally committed herself as a missionary in the conservative Missouri Synod Lutheran Church. A few years later, love set her life on another track and turned dreams of life in the mission field into dreams of an intercultural and interracial family. She convinced my father to move to a small farm and adopt children of various racial and ethnic backgrounds. I grew up with African American, Native American and Russian siblings; German exchange students; and a refrigerator papered over with pictures of World Vision–sponsored children in Africa and Latin America. Everything about the way my mom lived out her faith exemplified the connection between union with God and positive impact in the world.

When I was fifteen, my new church youth director changed the way I understood my call as a Christian in the world. She advocated a personal spiritual path inlaid with one's daily relationship with Jesus Christ. This idea of God as a personal friend and daily guide became a source of comfort and the catalyst for personal transformation: by coming to Jesus in honest prayer I could become my highest self. The joy of this discovery seemed to justify the call to share it with others—it was a call to give a gift that had changed my life. I became convinced that God was calling me to a life in Christian youth ministry, and I spent the next two summers at a youth ministry camp.

When I left home for Tanzania and Mt. Kilimanjaro, it was with a Baptist youth mission organization. I was strongly drawn to the vibrancy of praise and prayer within the Baptist church and moved more deeply also into its prioritization of evangelism. Yet, on the mountain, I struggled constantly with my role as an American evangelist. For the first time in my faith journey, I had a nagging sense of misdirection—a self-righteous isolationism that seemed contrary to Christian ideals of love and service. The question that emerged was essentially about how I as a Christian was called to relate to others of different spiritual groundings and different cultures. I began to question whether the ways that I was interacting with others were in fact leading to a positive transformation in the world.

I returned home and left for college, at a secular private school. In my freshman year I became the president of the largest religious group on campus, an evangelical Christian fellowship. I continued to grapple with the questions that had come up on Mt. Kilimanjaro. Though I tried to push these questions aside, they continually resurfaced as Christian friends tried to dissuade me from taking religion courses in the interest of protecting the purity of my faith, and budding relationships with new non-Christian friends died out whenever the topic of faith emerged.

I took the courses anyway and learned to quiet the evangelistic tones of my faith conversations. The next summer my experience with Burkut in Kazakhstan came in the midst of these questions. It challenged me directly to ponder not just how I interacted with non-Christians or questioning Christians, but with people of other religions. My senior year, an arson attack gutted a mosque in Minneapolis. I promoted efforts to help the mosque rebuild. I was met with sharp and immediate attack from members of the fellowship group and was asked to relinquish my leadership position. When I accepted an invitation by the college chaplain to join the newly formed Council for Religious Understanding, I found myself snubbed by some Christian friends and, by others, encouraged to use the opportunity to evangelize. I was arriving at a place of grand disillusionment with what I experienced as the Christian tradition.

Increasingly, I found myself horrified by divisive Christian rhetoric: "Muslims worship Satan; we all need Jesus; Hindus are heathen idol-worshipers; homosexuality is a sin; even if God made someone gay, the (cursed) person shouldn't act on it; Godly (Christian) men will save our world; man is the spiritual head of the woman."

I laid down my Bible. On attempts to pick it up again, I was continually overcome by a sickened sense of anger that had little to do with the scriptures themselves and everything to do with the way they had been used. My faith had grounded me all my life, and now I could hardly think the word "faith" without facing a deluge of rage. I reoriented myself by turning to the second element of my highest aspirations: being a positive force in the world. Union with God, as this concept had been taught to me, no longer seemed effective in meeting this goal. And so, I replaced prayer meetings and Bible studies with community organizing and youth work.

For two years, I threw myself into non–faith-based community building work, began casually studying non-Christian religions, and surrounded myself with mostly non-Christian friends. My work opened my eyes to the state of the world in which we live, to the reality of violence and oppression cut along lines of race, religion and ethnicity (I'm a small-town Minnesota girl). This was the context in which I would search for my calling. I was tormented by my work but, at the same time, glad to have found a guiding purpose. Still, even here I felt empty and unstable, shut off from the deepest part of who I was. I sensed that the "something missing" was my faith identity, and yet I didn't know how to reclaim it.

It was my deepening relationships with devotedly spiritual friends, both non-Christian and liberal Christian, and my reading of Christian activists like Dorothy Day, Martin Luther King Jr., and the interfaith Catholic theologian Thomas Merton that began to transform faith into a safe space for me once again. I gathered with friends to discuss books that grappled with the subject of faith and social justice. I went off to a retreat for spiritual activists and was fired up about the idea of Jesus as a revolutionary.

Then came an opportunity to work with the Interfaith Youth Core. Suddenly I was in the midst of organizing interfaith dialogues and action strategy meetings for young people of diverse faiths. I left every gathering with a deep sense of wholeness and joy. Prepared to face my Christian roots once again, I returned to church and opened myself back up to what I had thought was an adolescent whim, the call to go into ministry. This time, the call was stronger than ever, anchored in a lifelong commitment to interfaith peace building and a reinvigorated respect for my own faith tradition and the traditions of others.

My mom and I didn't often talk about God when I was growing up, but we have always shared a similar way of being in the world that is innately spiritual. The dreams that I now entertain are perhaps more progressive, as shaped by my immersion in a community of activists, but essentially they are the same—loving hospitality.

Two months ago I was sitting in the women's section of Al-Azhar Mosque in Cairo, praying silently. Another young woman, Egyptian, a couple of years my senior, sat down next to me and introduced herself as a local economist. She soon produced a gift for me—a set of books on Islam—and set about the task of persuading me that Christianity was an incomplete religion and that Islam offered me the whole truth. Her heavy-handed argument brought back memories of my own fervent evangelism and drew me into our commonality. I smiled, thanked her for her concern over my soul, and asked about her Christian, Hindu, and Buddhist friends.

A Muslim at the Catholic Worker

EBOO PATEL

I SPENT MY HIGH SCHOOL YEARS in suburban Chicago dreaming of the future comforts of fat paychecks. When I went to college at the University of Illinois in Champaign, I saw the other America—homeless Vietnam vets drinking mouthwash for the alcohol, minority students shunted to the back of overfull classrooms, battered women unable to find space at too-small shelters. I knew that America saw these shadows but chose not to call them. I did not want that disease.

So I flailed about wildly. I went to demonstrations and raged against the machine, but I did not see it improving anybody's life. I spent one summer living in communes and another traveling with the Grateful Dead, but decided escape wasn't my trip. I pierced my tongue and dressed in drag on campus, but realized that it wasn't a fashion revolution I was after. "Try being constructive," a professor advised me. So I started volunteering at shelters and schools, but I knew a broken world needed more than flimsy tape.

Few shared my frantic outlook. Most people were happy changing their clothes to fit the climate. Some folks left for places where the climate suited their clothes. A handful cursed the climate, shrugged, and went on their way. I wanted to change the climate. My loneliness was freezing.

Somebody said to me, "Go visit St. Jude's Catholic Worker house on the other end of town."

"What's a Catholic Worker house?" I asked.

"Part shelter for poor folks, part anarchist movement for Catholic radicals, part community for anyone who enters. Really, it's about a whole new way of living. You've got to go there to know."

From the moment I entered St. Jude's, it was clear to me that this was different from any other place I'd been. I couldn't figure out whether it was a shelter or a home. There was nobody doing intake. There was no executive director's office. White, black, and brown kids played together in the living room. I smelled food and heard English and Spanish voices coming from the kitchen. The first thing somebody said to me was, "Are you staying for dinner?" "Yes," I said.

The salad and stew were simple and filling, and the conversation came easy. After dinner, I asked someone, "Who is staff here? And who are the residents?"

"That's not the best way to think about this place," the person told me. "We're a community. The question we ask is 'What's your story?' There is a family here who immigrated from a small village in Mexico. The father found out about this place from his Catholic parish. They've been here for four months, enough time for the father to find a job and scrape together the security deposit on an apartment. There are others here with graduate degrees who believe that sharing their lives with the needy is their Christian calling. If you want to know the philosophy behind all of this, read Dorothy Day."

I did. And it made more sense to me than anything my Marxist professors lectured on, or my pre-law friends dreamed about, or my rock-and-roll records drove at. Recalling the thoughts of her college days, Dorothy wrote: "I did not see anyone taking off his coat and giving it to the poor. I didn't see anyone having a banquet and calling in the lame, the halt, and the blind. And those who were doing it, like the Salvation Army, did not appeal to me. I wanted life and I wanted the abundant life. I wanted it for others too."

Dorothy's vision of a culture of kindness was joined by a radical social outlook: "Why was so much done in remedying social evils instead of avoiding them in the first place? ... Where were the saints to try to change the social order, not just to minister to the slaves but to do away with slavery?"

Most importantly for me at the scowly-skeptical age of nineteen, Dorothy had lived her commitments in solidarity with the poor, not just ministering to them; she had lived in resistance to the system, with the jail time to prove it.

I spent a lot of time in Catholic Worker houses during my college years and early twenties. I cut carrots for the soup kitchen at Mary House in New York City, demonstrated at the Pentagon with Catholic Workers in Washington, D.C., even lived for a few weeks at the St. Francis House on the north side of Chicago. I marveled at Dorothy Day because she reimagined the world and lived her life in a way that created it anew. She called America's shadows to her dinner table, served them with love, and sat with them as a friend. It was the best antidote that I had seen for America's sickness.

And mine. Dorothy once said, "I'm working toward a world in which it would be easier for people to behave decently." I wanted to behave decently. The Catholic Worker was a chance to do justice for the marginalized and to achieve redemption for myself. Redemption meant being saved from the sickness of selfishness. Being cured meant joining humanity. And there was something transcendent in that.

It was at the Catholic Worker that I discovered a desire to touch the pure love of elsewhere. This was the love that Dorothy wrote about, the love that sourced and sustained her commitment. My faith journey was sparked not by a desire to enter heaven or from a fear of hell. It was neither about escape nor seclusion. I had no interest in the sin-and-
salvation kerosene of the religious right or the soupy spirituality of the New Age.

The faith I wanted would help me love and grieve and celebrate with all humanity. It would shape my eyes to see dignity and divinity in the dirty and ragged. I felt in my bones that humanity was meant for something more than we were achieving.

J. M. Coetzee says: "All creatures bring into this world the memory of justice." I knew that we had a purpose beyond providing for our own comfort. Abraham Joshua Heschel writes: "God is hiding in the world. Our task is to let the divine emerge from our deeds." I wanted to live the truth of June Jordan's vision: "I am a stranger / learning to worship the strangers / around me."

The religious life of the Catholic Worker inspired me. I loved the prayers for strength to do the work of justice. I found the Christian hymns and sermons elevating. I read the books of Worker heroes like Peter Maurin and Thomas Merton. But I always found myself standing at a slight angle to the central symbols of the Christian faith: the cross, the blood, the resurrection. And I never felt any desire to convert.

A short conversation with the leader of a Catholic Worker house in Atlanta was an important turning point in my faith journey. I asked if I could spend a summer working at his community. "Are you a Christian?" he asked. "No," I said. "Then it will be very difficult for you to take full part in the life of this community. Find a place where you fit, body and soul."

I understood his comment as an invitation, not an insult. It was time to find a faith home. I began reading across religious traditions. I read Ram Dass on Gandhi and Thich Nhat Hanh on the life of the Buddha. I found my head nodding to nearly every article of Bahai social teaching and felt as if I had discovered a gold mine when I came across the thought of the Jewish mystic Zalman Schachter. But my attraction to these traditions was intellectual. Similar to my experience with Christianity, I felt that my soul did not fit in any of them.

The one tradition that I did not explore was Islam, the religion I had been raised in. Islam was the tradition my parents carried with them when they left India. America was the situation that provided them with possibilities both stated and shrouded, opportunities that facilitated upward mobility but scattered centering values. My father was a successful advertising executive. My mother earned her CPA and began building a career. The ritual dimensions of Islam never fit comfortably into our American-style lives. We rarely attended Friday prayer and only occasionally gathered at home as a family to bow our heads to God. Still, we were Muslims. We did not eat pork. We said *Bismillah* when beginning new projects. We prayed *tasbi* during difficult times. And we helped people, especially Muslim immigrants, do everything from getting driver's licenses to earning advanced degrees.

Neglecting Islam was not so much a comment on the content of the religion as it was an adolescent habit of discriminating against the familiar. But, as James Baldwin writes, "Later, in the midnight hour, the missing identity aches."

I began a Buddhist (at least, what I thought was Buddhist) meditation practice when I was twenty-two. It consisted of sitting still and thinking about nothing. But the Ismaili Muslim mantra my mother whispered in my ear when I was a child—*Ya Ali, Ya Muhammad*—kept rising into my consciousness. In an attempt to stick to the program, I tried to push it out. Finally, it occurred to me that this was the program—I was a Muslim. My spiritual home had lived in my soul since my birth and before.

Later that year, I went to India to visit my grandmother. I woke up one morning to find a new person sitting on the sofa. She was barefoot and wearing a torn white nightgown several sizes too large for her.

"Who is she?" I asked my grandmother. "Call her Anisa. I don't know her real name," she told me. "Her father and uncle beat her, so she has come here. We will keep her safe."

My grandmother had been sheltering abused women for forty years by hiding them in her home. Those who are interested in education, she sends to school. For those who want to live with family in other parts of India, she pays for their travels. Others have just stayed and helped my grandmother around the house until they got married and started their own families. My grandmother has pictures of some of them, faded black-and-white shots, with pencil scribbles on the back telling the story.

After hearing the stories of about a dozen of these women, I wanted to know one more—my grandmother's. "Why do you do this?" I asked.

"Because I'm a Muslim. This is what Muslims do," she said.

My grandmother was a Muslim Dorothy Day. Her home had been a Muslim Catholic Worker. The heroes I was looking for were within my religion, in my very family.

I immersed myself in Islam. I sought examples of giants who had fought tyranny with love, and found them in Farid Esack and Badshah Khan. I desired beauty and found it in the poetry of Rumi and Ibn Arabi. I discovered the stories that revealed the grand purpose of humankind—that Allah made humanity *abd* and *khalifa*—Allah's servant and representative, on earth. I felt the truth of Islam in my soul—that Allah created Adam through the spirit in Allah's breath, that Allah chose Muhammad to be Prophet, and that Allah wanted me to submit to the will of Allah. I felt embraced by the compassion of Allah, forgiven by the mercy of Allah, and guided by the light of Allah.

I found full nourishment in Islam for ideas I initially encountered in other traditions. I am a Muslim whose first faith hero was Dorothy Day.

To Be a Mensch

HAROLD KASIMOW

I WAS BORN IN 1937 in a shtetl, a small village not far from Vilnius, Lithuania, which at that time was part of Poland. On July 2, 1941, just before my fourth birthday, the German army took control of our village. We lived under a traumatizing German occupation until April 3, 1942, when a priest informed my father of the massacre of the Jews in Braslov, a nearby village. This was our last chance to escape, and we did.

For the next several months my parents, my two older sisters, and I hid in barns and attics and many other places, helped by farmers in this area who risked their own lives to help us. When we all became sick with terrible coughs and could no longer hide near any home, my father dug a deep ditch in the forest, where we stayed for five weeks.

For the last nineteen months and five days before the war ended, my father excavated a tunnel underneath a stall in a barn that was next to the house of Wladislaw Piworowitz, a farmer he knew. We shared our underground hideout with mice, frogs, and worms. We also dug a small hole for defecation and urination. The entire time we were in the dark and did not wash. We were all infested with lice.

Throughout the war we lived in constant fear of being discovered by the Nazis or by others who would turn us in to the Nazis. On several occasions my family and I came very close to being found. Nearly all my relatives, including my mother's mother, with whom I had a special relationship, were murdered during the Holocaust.

These early experiences profoundly affected my life, which I have devoted to the study of the major religions of the world. I have been particularly attracted to saints, spiritual men and women of great compassion who are not preoccupied with themselves but with the suffering of other people, and who never adjust to violence but are free of it; they dedicate their lives to bringing compassion to the people of our planet. I have been fortunate to meet many such extraordinary men and women from different religious traditions. They have had a great impact on me.

Foremost among them was my teacher Abraham Joshua Heschel, whom I first met at the Jewish Theological Seminary in New York City when I was nineteen years old. What stands out for me the most during the five years that I studied at the seminary was my unique relationship with Professor Heschel, with whom I had a course on Genesis, emphasizing Rashi's interpretation, and a course on Jewish theology, in which we read Heschel's classic work, *God in Search of Man*. At the time I thought that the reason for my special relationship with Heschel was due to the fact that we were both Holocaust survivors and that we sometimes conversed in Yiddish, which was our birth language. I now know that there were other students who were strongly attracted to Heschel, not only because he had a brilliant mind but also because he was a real mensch. This Yiddish word for "human being" signifies someone who is truly human, a compassionate being of dignity and great integrity. A mensch is a person who combines compassion with a passion for truth.

Today Heschel is admired as the greatest spiritual Jewish teacher and activist of the twentieth century. But already in the 1950s and 1960s, a few of his students came to see him as the saint of our generation. In recent years I have offered a seminar titled "Abraham Joshua Heschel: A Jewish Saint of the Twentieth Century." His teaching of Judaism stirred the hearts and minds of Jews and Christians because he incorporated into his own system of thought the insights of both the ethical and the mystical streams of the Jewish tradition.

I was most drawn to Heschel's stress on the ethical dimension of Judaism, which aims at ethical perfection, the total transformation of the human being. It is an emphasis on *aggadah*, that is, spirituality, not just on *halakhah*, that is, law. In *aggadah* the focus is on what is in the heart of the believer while he or she fulfills the demands of God, not only on the doing of the deed itself. Heschel believed that the goal of Judaism was to create a harmony between *halakhah* and *aggadah*. For him, the ethical aspect of Judaism is as important as the ritualistic.

Heschel also believed that a pious person has to be as mindful of relations with other human beings as of the relationship with God. According to Heschel, we must be "alert to the dignity of every human being." He writes that the pious person is "keenly sensitive to pain and suffering in our own life and in that of others." In his book on the Jews of Eastern Europe, *The Earth Is the Lord's*, Heschel gives the following definition of a saint: "A saint was he who did not know how it is possible not to love, not to help, not to be sensitive to the anxiety of others."

There are certainly many reasons why Heschel's students were drawn to him. In my own case I believe it was my early experiences that so strongly attracted me to him and his work. As in other traditional Jewish families in Lithuania, my parents valued scholarship and did not question the legal aspect of the tradition, but they also placed a strong emphasis on the ethical aspect. What was most important to them was the character of the people they encountered. The critical question for them was whether a person was a real mensch. Like other Lithuanian Jews, my parents were exposed to the teachings of Rabbi Israel Salanter, who founded the Musar Movement, a self-perfection movement, in Vilnius in the 1840s. He devoted his life to guiding Jews on a path to ethical perfection, to the transformation of the individual. A great Talmudic scholar, Salanter believed that the study of Talmud by itself was not enough to free a person from selfishness. He was convinced that in order to bring about a transformation, one must also immerse oneself in the great Jewish ethical texts, such as Rabbi Bahya Ibn Paquda's *The Duties of the Heart* and Rabbi Moses Hayyim Luzzatto's

The Path of the Righteous. Luzzatto's work became particularly precious to the Musar Movement. Many students learned by heart its clearly developed path that leads one step by step to the stage of human perfection.

Although Salanter claimed that "It is more difficult to change a single character trait than to cover the entire Talmud," he felt that the study of such Musar texts with one's whole being would lessen egoism and would ultimately lead to the transformation of the individual. He once said that the truly great wonder in the world is that it is possible "to transform a human being into a mensch." That was the most important message I learned from my parents: one must be a mensch.

In their visions of the Jewish tradition, I see a strong affinity between Heschel, who studied in Vilnius for two years, and Salanter. In a well-known interview with Carl Stern, Heschel directed the following message to young people: "And above all, remember that the meaning of life is to build a life as if it were a work of art.... Start working on this great work of art called your own existence." To work on oneself is also the central message of Salanter and the Lithuanian Musar Movement he founded. I believe that my early influences at home and my three years as a student at Yeshiva Israel Salanter in the Bronx, where my parents enrolled me soon after we arrived in the United States in 1949, helped to draw me to Professor Heschel.

I cannot describe here the many other incredible people from different religious traditions whom I have encountered in my life. I do, however, want to express my deep gratitude and love to Lolya Lipchitz, the woman to whom I have been married for over twenty-five years. Without having studied at a Musar yeshiva, she is my living Musar teacher, who has committed her life to *tikkun olam,* "healing the world."

Finding Harmony in the Spiritual Journey

JEFF GENUNG

I WAS BORN INTO A Roman Catholic home. My mother and grand-mother, both of whom were devout Catholics, influenced my early years. My Catholic school education made religion part of my daily life. At about the age of ten, I began a period of deep inquiry into some of the tenets of my faith. I pondered questions like these: Who am I? What is my purpose in life? Who and what is God? Why is there something instead of nothing? What is the purpose of it all? I asked these questions of many influential adults and religious people in my life.

The answers that I received from them gave me a distinct feeling of uneasiness, as if maybe they really didn't know the answers to these great questions. It felt as if they were telling me what they believed or what they had been told, but their answers didn't seem to come from a place that was grounded in their own personal experiences.

The realization that maybe nobody really knows the truth about these matters came to me as somewhat of a delightful shock. It was my first real feeling of liberation. It occurred to me that if no one really knows the answers to these great questions, then I might as well begin my own journey of discovery and ask the universe myself. My spiritual journey really began consciously at that moment.

After six years of intense self-inquiry, wondering, and deep prayer, a spiritual breakthrough occurred. By God's grace I was granted a deep and lasting experience that revealed something profound about the nature of the self, God, and existence. This single experience forever altered my views about God, humankind, nature, religion, and the cosmos. I was given a brief glimpse of the underlying unity, consciousness, and love that connects all of cosmic existence. From that time on I have had a profound sense of the connectedness of us all.

This experience of the grace of the Divine, which was to forever change my life, occurred during a discussion I was having with a friend about the true nature of the self and the ego. We were discussing and pondering this matter with great wonder and fervor, when all of a sudden my awareness, the feeling of the "I" presence, left my body and somehow beheld its own image. I could see the self in greater reality and detail than if I had been looking in a mirror. This event began a process that altered all my previous and future perceptions about everything. There was a realization that neither I, nor anyone else, was really who or what I previously thought they were. A period of clear seeing, feeling, and knowing followed for many days. During this time, I experienced an unusually heightened degree of awareness, resulting in a variety of profound experiences.

As a boy I lived in the country and spent a good deal of time in nature. During this period of heightened awareness I went deep into the woods and sat in silent meditation for many hours. I was in a state of profound prayer, feeling the unity of human beings, nature, and the cosmos and the presence of the Holy Spirit. When I opened my eyes again they fell on a deer that was observing and drawing nearer. I then looked and saw a turkey and then a squirrel, hawk, rabbit, birds, and other creatures. As I turned my head I could see that I was surrounded with different kinds of wildlife. I sensed that we were each deeply aware of one another's presence, and that we were all witnessing a great mystery. With this expanded awareness, it felt as if the very sap coursing through the heartwood of the trees and the blood coursing through each of the creatures' veins were my very own blood. As I looked at the canopy above and saw the sun reflect off the leaves and as the wind moved each leaf as if in a coordinated dance, I could see, feel, know, and understand that somehow everything is alive and communicating. There was an awareness that everything, by the fact of its very existence, has meaning and purpose, and that it is part of an underlying unity of conscious love.

It wasn't until some years later that I crossed paths with a man who was to become my first real teacher. Upon first meeting him I instinctively knew that he possessed a genuine understanding about the nature of God and the mystical life. I did not fully know that working with him would lead me to be part of a community that made into a living reality the sense of unity and harmony that I had felt in the forest.

At the time I met him, Tim Cook was about to embark on a five-year experiment in Christian community. Tim was an ordained Christian minister but had also spent time in ashrams in India working with teachers from other traditions. Tim and his wife, Barbara, hungered to work with others who were serious about the spiritual life and transformation—people who were committed to making daily spiritual practice the center of their lives. With this shared intention of a community of disciplined spiritual practitioners, the Church of Conscious Harmony was formed.

It has now been fifteen years since that small group of people first gathered. The Church of Conscious Harmony has become a vibrant community of some three hundred householders who are simultaneously disciplined practitioners. It is a community of adults, youth, and children who live the contemplative life—ordinary people leading a deeply devotional life and living out of God's extraordinary love.

The bylaws of this church state that the church honors all other spiritual traditions and is open to using any teachings and practices that can broaden and deepen our own Christian experience and understanding. The theological foundation of the church is rooted in two ancient sources:

1. The contemplative dimension of the Gospel and Centering Prayer as taught by Fr. Thomas Keating.

2. The esoteric Christian tradition of transformative psychology otherwise known as The Work, as passed down through the teachings of G. I. Gurdjieff and through Eastern Orthodoxy.

Over the last thirteen years The Church of Conscious Harmony has been host to a virtual banquet of wise spiritual teachers from a variety of traditions, including Tibetan lamas and rinpoches; monks, nuns and priests; *sannyāsa*; rabbis; and other experts in the areas of spiritual psychology, sacred dance, mysticism, and Centering Prayer. It is a very ecumenical community that truly respects and honors all other religious and spiritual traditions while remaining deeply rooted in its own ancient tradition. This is a community that understands and is receptive to the treasures that exist within each of the world's religions. Our deeply rooted faith in our own tradition enables us to welcome and receive other faiths without sacrificing our own or imposing ours on another.

As a community we have learned from the wisdom, knowledge, and practices of many other traditions. For instance, we have benefited from the deep connection to nature and Earth that exists in the Native American tradition. We have learned from the profound mysticism of the Hindu Upanishads and the love poetry and sacred dances of the Sufi mystics. We have developed our own form of devotional chanting that we have learned from spending time in ashrams and listening to bajans and listening to Gregorian chants in Christian monasteries. We have learned about dying and the stages of death from the Tibetan tradition. We have learned about the value of silence and solitude from the Christian and Buddhist monastic traditions.

The children in our community have been taught from an early age to honor and respect other faiths, religions, and beliefs. Both the adults and the youth of this community realize that people of other faiths need not be feared or misunderstood. Indeed, our diversity can be part of the gift that we offer to one another as human beings. Our differences can be culturally and spiritually nourishing to us even as we learn and grow in our own tradition. By respecting the wisdom and beauty of other religious traditions, including their holy books, rites, rituals, and practices, we actually enlarge our own understanding of the Divine. By accepting other traditions with open minds and open hearts, we can see how the Divine works through different individuals, cultures, and traditions to reveal the Divine Reality, to reveal the essence of humankind to each other, and to reveal the true nature of each human to himself or herself.

Another living insight about the importance of the interfaith experience came as I was working with a group of young people at our church. They began asking me questions about other religions: Why are there so many different religions? How are they similar and how do they differ? There happened to be a prism in the room. The idea came to me to use it as a metaphor for communicating the essence of what interspirituality means. I held the prism up to the light, and we looked at the different colors. We observed the different colors of the rainbow and discussed how each line of color was unique and different and yet how each of the colors is related to the others. We could all see and understand how the colors blend one into another and yet how each line could be followed back to a common source of white light. We were all struck by the utter simplicity of it all and could see how the divine spirit might work in a similar way with the human family in matters of religious diversity.

We all come from different cultures with different languages, customs, and religious traditions, but yet we are all human. Each of us has been graced with a unique outer form that differs in color, size, shape, and personality, and yet we are all commonly alive as heart, mind, body, and spirit. We all suffer, and we all long to be happy. Indeed, we all spring from the same vine of life, without which none of us can live for even a moment. The colors of the rainbow are like the different religious traditions. Each band of the color spectrum is unique and beautiful in its own right and serves a specific purpose. In the same way, each person and each tradition serves as an extension of the divine presence. What would a rainbow be without all of the colors represented? Each religious tradition is unique, precious, beautiful, and filled with purpose and meaning. Each genuine religious tradition springs from the Divine

Source.

Our community has experienced the fruit that comes through religious and spiritual dialogue. Our young people and children have a natural acceptance and understanding of other religious traditions. We embrace and celebrate our differences. Many of the spiritual leaders who have shared with us over the years have commented on how honored they feel that a Christian church should be so welcoming, reverent, and honoring of their traditions.

The interspiritual life of the Church of Conscious Harmony has been an opportunity for me to help manifest on earth the truth of the harmony that I experienced with all of divine creation that day as a young man in the forest. I am a simple householder and family man, not a scholar or religious professional. However, I realize more and more that interspirituality belongs to us all. As such, it is everyone's right and responsibility to share his or her experience of this emerging reality. Interspirituality is ultimately as diverse as humanity itself, and therefore everyone's views and experience on this subject can be both useful and valid.

The experience of finding common ground among the traditions may be a rarity today, but it is part of a growing global movement that is just now in its infancy. The interspiritual movement is a participation of the natural maturing process of the human family. Our humanity is beginning to mature into our divinity. We are at the very cusp of a worldwide spiritual movement that many will embrace, some may fear, yet none will stop.

I believe that interspirituality offers us a genuine hope for the future and provides us with an expanded vision for the human family. It incorporates and yet transcends the religious, cultural, and personal boundaries that have been both the foundation of our respective faiths and yet have also served as barriers to a more universal understanding of humanity's fundamental unity of spirit.

The Gift

JULIET BERIOU

S OMEHOW I FELT HER TERROR. As she glanced away from me I felt the desperation lurking behind her proud face. She was young and alone, alone with a child.

Was it her fault? She had had an affair with my husband—her boss. My world had been rocked. It had been like finding out there is no God. No God, *no nothing*. My heart had been instantly seared into nothingness. No more feeling. No more belief. No more. I never knew that life could end so swiftly and totally, even as I went on driving the kids to school and nodding to my colleagues. I never knew I would lie on my living room floor writhing in pain, screaming inwardly, vaguely aware that I was being crucified without anyone noticing.

I couldn't even tell anyone. Something inside me said, "Don't throw it away. Get through it for the girls, if nothing else." If I talked about it, he'd lose his job, his referrals, probably have to leave the state. It was up to me.

He was sorry, but bizarre, wanted to send her to college. He "owed her something." Send her to college? Us, with three children to educate? He wanted me to be nice to her. Of course. Anything else?

So I poured my pain into my journal and wept in the predawn light, and sobbed against the living room wall until I slowly fell exhausted to the floor. I listened to him as he unloaded. Accompanied him to the therapist, and listened more. I moved through the suffocating fog of the day somehow. I had children to think of. He had, until now, been a good father. He had, until now, been a good man.

So here we were, walking into his office to meet with her. She wanted to know where she stood. Was she going to be fired? Was I going to "tell"? After all, he and I had each other to get through this. She had no one. Indeed. Who was better off?

I was numb. My face and throat were plastic coated. My eyes burned like a lighted gasoline slick. Walking into that office, I felt my skin go cold. My heart raged. I will speak. By God, *I will speak.*

I threw my coat on a chair and glared at both of them as they slunk to separate corners. He looked pathetic. She was so small. She wasn't even pathetic. She was smaller than that. It was as if even her soul had abandoned her—a papery shell that tried to do "defiant," but could barely manage a "no."

I stared at her for what seemed like hours and slowly began to really see her. It was all there in her face: the abandonment, the desperation, the hopelessness. She had sold herself. Sold her very soul. And she had been swindled.

"Kristy," I murmured. "Kristy ..."

My voice went soft as I pulled my chair closer. "You are worthy of so much more."

She threw a startled glance at me before staring again at the floor. "I never meant to hurt you or the girls." She coughed. "I need you to know that."

"I do know that," I said. "I know that now. And I know a lot more too." I paused, half-alarmed at the sudden absence of my heartbeat. "I know that you are good."

She tossed me a quick look through narrowed eyes.

"I mean it. You are good. What happened was not good, but that isn't who you are. You're so much more than that, and you deserve so much more. You deserve to love and be loved fully and freely. Loved for who you are, the beautiful being that you are."

My body relaxed and I felt light, almost flooded by light. "It's time for you to live out who you are. Enough of the fear. Enough of the settling. You're so much more than that, and I can see it. It's time to believe in your dreams, and to live them out. You have the spirit to do it, Kristy, and it's time."

"I can't believe you're saying this to me," she said.

I drew in a breath. "I see who you are. You are good. You're full of goodness. It's time to claim it."

I waited.

Her eyes met mine, this time without the fear.

She shook her head and blinked. "I don't get it. I thought you were going to ream me out. I mean I deserve it. I practically destroyed your life."

"No one can destroy my life except me," I said. "And no one can destroy yours. Now is the time to claim your life for yourself. Take it and create what you want, what you deserve. Don't settle for what you've had in the past. It's time, Kristy. It's yours." I leaned over and touched her arm. "Kristy, you *are* good."

She put her cold fingers on my hand and almost smiled. "I can't believe this."

"It's time to believe it," I said feeling my heart restart. "It's time to start living."

She half-nodded and gazed at the ceiling before turning to him. "You don't deserve her. You don't now, and you never did."

I didn't feel cold as he and I walked out into that December night.

He let out a low whistle "I can't believe what just happened in there. It was like the scene from *Les Miserables* when the bishop helps the guy who stole from him."

I shook my head and looked up at the suddenly sharp stars. "Don't give me any credit. I'm not that good. That was *la de arriba*. That was from God."

Yes, it was one more instance of learning to listen, and to really hear. For many years I had walked around oblivious to the workings of the gift · 31

God in my life and to the way events presented themselves or unfolded. "Coincidence," I used to mutter.

It seemed God had to be a bit more compelling with me. First, God planted a knowing in my heart that had me uproot the whole family and go off to serve the poor in Mexico for a year. Everyone went kicking and screaming, but it turned out to be the richest experience of each of their lives. God dramatically saved me from a near-death experience in El Salvador, imparting the lesson that we are not in control. Then God held me up during my divorce, when I thought I was truly going to die from the pain. Actually I did die, in a certain way, but holding that connection to the Knowing resurrected me and made me stronger than ever.

Most recently, it was a call to uproot my life again and move to downtown Chicago—where I had no family or friends, no job, no contacts. I left behind my home and friends of twenty years and went to live in an urban landscape in some ways more foreign to me than Mexico.

Living in open connection to the Divine has taken the fear out of life. Instead of cringing and whispering, "I wonder what's going to come next?" I have opened my eyes, looked at the horizon, and murmured, "I wonder what's coming next?"

To listen with wonder, to live life with one's hands outstretched and one's heart open: those are the fruits of choosing to receive the Divine connection that's continually being offered. It is a choice. It is our choice. It is a way to freedom, and to peace.

Now, when I relate to people, I find myself seeing beyond their personality structure, with all the often-irritating behaviors and unconsciousness actions. I find myself seeing them as perfect, light-filled beings, here for a special purpose. I feel a special kinship with almost everyone, and I look at them wondering what are their challenges in this life and what are their special life lessons. I often feel, as Thomas Merton described on that street corner in Kentucky, union with them all—even the ones who cause problems for me in my life. I see us all as companions on the path, all trying our best given our context, and

I have lost interest in judging or even interpreting others' actions. We are all crossing the same river to the same destination—we are just crossing in different boats.

I find I have frequent attacks of smiling and appreciation. I don't worry much, and I have an increased tendency to let things happen rather than to try to make them happen. Fear seems to have receded into a memory, and when it does present itself, I ask it what it is here to teach me and step out into it, knowing I will come out the other side enriched and transformed.

Given my life circumstances, most would conclude that I should be afraid to trust—especially in extensions of love by others—but I'm not. In fact, I find myself living more and more from an openhearted place, and freely responding to the love extended by others. The most tangible effect of choosing to live in the flow of divine connection, though, is the overwhelming urge to extend love to others. Some may call it fool-hardy, but I wouldn't want to live this life any other way. I have received a gift—granted that it arrived on the shoulders of intense suffering—but I chose to say yes to the gift, and I have never been the same. Gratitude is what I breathe as I wake up in the morning, as I go to work, and as I dance tango and eat tuna fish sandwiches. Life is still full of the mundane and the routine, but it is also sublime. I find meaning in every-thing, and know that we are *all* in it together.

One Small Step Can Change Your Life

Desmond Papi Oganne

W HEN I WAS A YOUNG BOY growing up in a township in South Africa, there was nothing to make me different from the other boys. There would have been a difference only if I had grown up differently: say, in the rich, wealthy suburbs of Johannesburg rather than the dusty mine dumps of Soweto.

I was the last child in a family of five children—three sisters and a brother. We were a staunch Christian family. This didn't make a difference in how I looked at life, or how I related to others who were different from me in color, gender, or culture. Our parents had lived in an intercultural community, but they were forcibly removed, and separated by culture. As children we grew up with that division.

Like any other child, I had anger and did not care about white or any other culture. This made me look only at those of my own culture and those who lived around me. I was not exposed to the white culture, and even today my exposure is limited. Blacks today generally interact with whites only because of work. I am still living with the assumptions of the South African white culture.

My eldest sister and my brother are very political, and I am the same. I was very political at school, but the funny thing is that my parents had no idea about this, and I did not let them know. They thought I was different from my brother and sister, which was good.

Things came to a point of change in my life. A white priest had visitors from Germany. He had served in our local church, and even before coming there, he had served in other black community churches. To this day I don't even have a clue why he never worked in the white community.

One day he asked me to take him and his guests around the township. What he saw in me I had no idea at that time. I thought, "Here is another white man using a young black boy." But I discovered that things were not like that. He invited me to his house and then went further, saying "You can live with us if you want to."

Maybe you are thinking as you read this, "There is a black boy grabbing a chance." In a way it is true, but the chance was that I began to learn something about white culture. I still had in the back of my head that there weren't really any good whites.

While staying with the priest and his guests, I was introduced to conflict resolution. At first I thought, "Is this really another way to solve our conflicts, or just another skill to use?" It turned out that the whole experience changed my personality. I am more open to learning about other cultures—not only the culture of white South Africa, but others around the globe. This has given me a chance to work with people in different countries. To make things even more interesting, I worked with people in North Belfast, Northern Ireland. From some of the children coming from other countries, cultures and families in conflict and violence, I learned to listen to their stories—to sympathize, empathize, console, and be compassionate.

One small step can change your life. A simple act can change the life of the next person—a small bit of talk. Being there can comfort someone. Patience and mercy—that's what we need to make Earth a better planet to live in.

Fulfilling the Heart's Deepest Longing

LAMA PALDEN DROLMA

> Wisdom is
>
> sweeter than honey,
>
> brings more joy
>
> than wine,
>
> illumines
>
> more than the sun,
>
> is more precious
>
> than jewels.
>
> She causes
>
> the ears to hear
>
> and the heart to comprehend.
>
> —Makeda, Queen of Sheba, excerpted from
> *Women in Praise of the Sacred*, edited by Jane Hirshfield

WHILE I WAS GROWING UP, my family belonged to the Episcopalian parish nearby. From the age of eight years, I sang in the choir. The liberal attitude of Californian Anglicans emphasized love and kindness in daily life, and prayer and communion in services. From my parents, and supported by the teachings of the church, I believed that we were meant to help others less fortunate than ourselves, that we stood for peace and understanding among all peoples. I was taught to value different races and traditions. Singing in the choir gave my naturally very devotional personality a wonderful stream within which to manifest. The church's open atmosphere with its lack of spiritual judgment and condemnation allowed me to enter in a child's way into mystical union during Holy Communion. Of course, at the time, I didn't think of it in those terms; it was a natural, uncontrived, spontaneous process that I didn't think much about. I simply enjoyed it.

When I was thirteen years of age, everything shifted. The worldview that I had lived in was shattered by the reality of the Vietnam War and by the forces of unhappiness and discontent that led to the breakup of both my own family and the families of every one of my close friends within a short time. The Vietnam War rudely awakened me to the fact that our government and indeed many Americans, including many in our own congregation, were not for international peace and brotherhood. My naivete was broken, and I was deeply dismayed. I left the church, because to my thirteen-year-old way of thinking, many of the church members were hypocritical to the values I had thought the church stood for. Not until I was older was I able to separate out the pure stream of Christianity from the views of certain church members.

At the same time, as a freshman in high school, I had a dynamic, inspirational teacher for humanities. In his class we studied Huston Smith's *Religions of Man* as well as the leading writers in psychology at the time, such as Fritz Perls, Eric Fromm, and Eric Berne. During our studies of Islam, I was very taken with the idea of praying to Mecca five times a day, and I talked my best friend into doing this practice with me for a brief period of time.

But the most profound influence on me at this time—one that I was exposed to by the War Resisters League—was Mahatma Gandhi. As a fourteen-year-old I read and studied Gandhi enthusiastically. I fully embraced his teachings on *ahimsa* (nonviolence) and nonviolent resistance. His stance of honoring and working with people of all the religions of India seemed to me to be obviously correct. I naturally had a deep love for all religious traditions. When I was about ten or eleven, my maternal grandmother, to whom I was very close, had given me two small books of wisdom sayings: one a compilation from the Far East and one from the Christian tradition. I especially loved the Eastern one and would pore over it, absorbing, to the best of my ability, the poetic teachings of ancient great masters.

In the summer of my fifteenth year, I volunteered at "Vietnam Summer," a project to help end the war. This was a seminal experience for me, because I realized that war manifests in the world because of the anger and aggression that lives inside each of us. I quit volunteering and decided to concentrate on rooting out the anger and conflicts within myself. During my junior and senior years in high school, I realized that, much like my father, a Type A business executive, I was tense, with a kind of tightly coiled energy. It was difficult for me to relax and just be with myself. Although I lived in one of the most beautiful places in the world, the Tiburon hills, and had every opportunity available to me as well as loving, supportive parents, I was not happy. I felt that I would need to learn to calm my mind and relax if I was going to be able to enjoy my life. Yet, even though I had learned to meditate during a semester at a Quaker school in northern California, I was not yet psychologically ready to actually take on my "monkey mind" and meditate regularly. Meditation didn't really stick with me until my twenty-second year, when I began a committed daily practice of both Za-zen and hatha yoga. At the time, I was thoroughly enjoying studying comparative religion in college, and I knew intuitively that in order to cut through my neurotic habit patterns (which were quite obvious at least in their superficial characteristics), I needed to engage in both physical and mental spiritual practices.

Suzuki Roshi's disciple Bill Kwong, a San Francisco native, had established a zendo in the Sonoma Mountains among the vineyards. I began to study Buddhism and to sit Za-zen with him. His lectures were fascinating, but I didn't understand anything of what he said. However, the practice felt absolutely right, even though it wasn't easy. As the morning sun hit the grapevine leaves surrounding the zendo, they glowed a luminescent green. My mind felt cleansed and refreshed after the sitting meditation. But although I very much appreciated and learned from Bill Kwong, I didn't feel that Zen was my home, and I didn't feel that he was to be my teacher in the sense of coming to rest there with him in practice and study. I did continue to sit Za-zen, however.

The following year I moved back to Marin, where I had grown up. I had also been exploring Christian mysticism, and at this time I went back to the church I had been raised in, joined the choir, and reconnected with the true stream of Christian blessing. I continued my studies in comparative religion at the local Dominican college. A chance meeting with another young mother brought me into contact with the Bay Area Sufi community that was part of the Chisti Order. This lineage was brought to America in the early part of the twentieth century by Hazrat Inayat Khan, a great mystic and teacher from India. I began studying with one of his disciples, Murshida Vera. At the time, near the end of her working life, she was running a Sufi school for children aged four to seven, and teaching Sufi practices and philosophy to adults. Emotional healing happened for me during this time, both from the Sufi practices—which emphasize opening the heart; attuning oneself to love, harmony, and beauty; and honoring all religions—and from the reconnection with Christianity. In both these traditions I was again singing in praise to the Divine—a practice that had opened the door of sacred connection for me as a child. I was again in the choir at church, and in the Sufi community I joined in the "Dances of Universal Peace" that had been created by another disciple of Inayat Kahn's: Murshid Sam Lewis. This was deeply satisfying, but I still felt that I had not yet met my teacher. So I began to pray continually that I would meet my teacher, walking over to what I called the Mary Garden, near my home. This was, at the time, an overgrown, untended garden at the Dominican convent, which had a lovely statue of the Virgin Mary. I prayed to Mary to connect me with my teacher.

One day, a Sufi-Buddhist friend of mine stopped by the house to cajole me into coming with him to hear a great Tibetan master speak in San Francisco. After a hard sell from him, I agreed to go. Five minutes after walking into the old school gymnasium and seeing and hearing this old master, I knew that he was my teacher. I had an immediate physical reaction to him—my nose began to run, and I started coughing, even though I wasn't sick at the time. This master was Kalu Rinpoche. It was the full moon in September 1977. I thought that whatever religion he belonged to was fine because I felt such a deep and profound connection with him. Later in the evening he offered to give refuge to those who wanted it. Taking refuge is a formal Buddhist ceremony somewhat akin to baptism in the Christian faith, except that Kalu Rinpoche always said that if one wasn't Buddhist, one could take refuge and not give up one's own religion. He felt that the benefits of refuge would go with you wherever your spiritual journey took you.

Since those first few minutes when I realized that Kalu Rinpoche was my teacher, my complete confidence and devotion to him has never wavered. I have had the great good fortune to meet many realized masters whose teachings and kindness I am very grateful for, as they have each and every one greatly benefited me. Yet, for me, finding the one I call my teacher—or what they call in Tibetan one's root guru—completely changed my life.

I soon began doing the foundational practices from the Kagyu Buddhist tradition, a Vajrayana or Tibetan Buddhist lineage. From the time I met Kalu Rinpoche, profound blessing has manifested in my life. A deep shift occurred almost immediately in my daily meditation practice when I began to include a dedication of merit. This is a prayer done by all Tibetan Buddhists at the end of a meditation session that dedicates any benefit accrued by the practice to the alleviation of suffering and full awakening of all sentient beings. Somehow, adding the element of dedication to my practice in a positive way disentangled my practice from my sense of self and empowered it.

The path wasn't by any means all easy. During the first eight years after meeting Rinpoche and taking refuge with him, I did a lot of meditation practice and study, going through purification and transformation. I traveled to Darjeeling, India, to study with him and with other masters, including the late H.H. the sixteenth Gyalwa Karmapa. In 1982 I entered a completely cloistered retreat lasting three years and three months. Here I was trained in the traditional way of meditation and philosophy, which included chanting, praying, visualization practices, yoga, and music.

My youngest brother died at age twenty-seven during the last year of my retreat. The pain of his passing overtook me and threw me into a crisis. My emotional, psychological, and family values screamed at me to leave the retreat in order to be with my family. It is not possible to leave a three-year retreat and come back in. My teacher reminded me of my commitment to stay in retreat for the appointed time; non-verbally I felt his communication to me to deal with the totality of the situation from a much bigger spiritual perspective.

I turned everything to the path as best as I could. This means looking at whatever difficulties arise as opportunities to apply the methods of the Dharma. Continually praying to my lama and all the awakened beings, surrendering to ultimate truth, I was held through a kind of death process. Eventually, through the blessing, the Absolute—or what we might call the vast, empty, omnipresent awareness—opened within me. The core of my pain at my brother's death gave way and was released, and a deep spiritual joy emerged. Somehow, I feel that my deep transformational process was of benefit to my brother and family as well. Both my parents later told me that they were glad I had stayed and completed the retreat rather than coming out at the time of the funeral.

Directly after the retreat, I felt that my heart had reconnected with itself. The deep spiritual longing that had compelled me since I was a teenager was consummated into mystical union. This has never left me.

I had been trained to be a lama (a role similar to that of a priest, rabbi, or roshi). One year after completing the retreat, I was able to see my root lama, Kalu Rinpoche. In December 1986, when I saw Rinpoche, he named me as a lama of the Kagyu and Shangpa lineages. Since that time I have taught Buddhist meditation and philosophy.

The transformation that occurred allowed me to access the Divine. Experiences manifested both spontaneously and in practice. I still had much work to do, both internally and externally, but my deepest heart's longing had been fulfilled.

Awakening

Spencer Perdriau

Only when you have experienced the lowest of the lowest are you then humbled enough to appreciate and experience The Highest of The Highest.

As a young boy I always had a strong belief in God, but I didn't actually *realize* God till I was twenty-three. I grew up under the Western structures of the Christian faith, but my family was not heavily influenced by the tradition or dogma of Christianity, and we did not even attend a regular church service, only (rarely) the Christmas mass service. In a way, I was rather fortunate not to be confined and restricted to the traditions or dogma of any one particular faith, for it allowed me to freely investigate and develop my own understanding and belief in God through my own young capacity, experience, and insights. However, the accuracy of my personalized adolescent opinions and beliefs would not be realized, clarified, and corrected until I hit my early twenties.

Before my teenage years I was very happy, open, carefree, and outgoing. Then in my teenage years I became rather quiet and introspective, very much a contemplative individual. When I turned twenty, I encountered a very traumatic situation regarding my college sweetheart, which caused me to take a turn for the worst. Feeling that it was too much to bear, I suffered from a mental breakdown. I was diagnosed with an episode of schizophrenia. At the time, stress gave way to anxiety, anxiety gave way to paranoia, and paranoia then gave way to a horrific fall into a catatonic state of psychosis. It was an extremely uncomfortable hell, full-time for me, and although at the time I did not know that I was suffering from the illness called schizophrenia, I definitely knew right from the very start that something was seriously wrong with me. This was not who I was supposed to be. At the time, I experienced schizophrenia (psychosis) for about a week and a half, with a climax period featuring auditory hallucinations lasting for about half a day. I have never again had hallucinations.

It took a good ten months to recover from this initial episode. I went through a period of heavy depression before finding my foundations again. Since that first experience I have encountered three more mild relapses, each lasting no longer than two to three weeks. These brief encounters featured very scary associations and ideas of reference. Once recovered from that initial nightmare state in my life, I began seriously to question how and why the mind can act in such a devastating, destructive way. I also began to develop a tenacious pursuit to understand what consciousness *really* is. Fortunately for me, my first psychiatrist specialized in transpersonal psychology and was associated with the School of Philosophy for many years. I visited my doctor every Thursday afternoon, and instead of him counseling me, we would freely and eagerly discuss the nature of consciousness. I even remember how our very first conversation started: I asked him, "Is consciousness produced from the brain or does the brain just house it for use and operation?" And from there, my real spiritual journey began.

During this time my doctor gave me a copy of the Bhagavad Gita for my birthday, the very beautiful navy-blue two-volume commentary translation by Paramahansa Yogananda, and I couldn't put it down. Reading Yogananda's translations of these Eastern scriptures helped me begin to develop a clearer understanding and appreciation for Western scripture, particularly the pure essence of the Christian faith. So, the weeks passed. As a result of reading the scriptures and my very eager attendance with my doctor each week, my awareness was becoming more and more in awe of the greater reality of existence that was being presented to me. Not only was I feeling great joy from such discussions, so was my doctor. I had very much fallen deeply in love with the nature of God, and God Itself. Then one day a few months later, it all came to a mass, when I was struck—totally out of the blue—with a very brief, yet very intense experience of nonduality, lasting for about ten seconds. Within that time, I felt (and I stress the word "felt") no difference between my immediate self and everything around and beyond me. The difference between here and there was gone. It was as if my individual boundaries had been lost and nothing distinguished me from all else.

It all happened when I was attending to my usual training at the local gym. Resting between a set of exercises, I stood there, paused in silence, breathing deeply and smoothly, coming to a complete halt. Looking up slightly, I became still within myself, and in that moment, the gym all of a sudden became quiet to me, and I felt myself go. I began to feel myself larger than my ordinary physical size, larger than my individuality. My boundaries of personality instantly gave way (dissolved), and I felt myself expanding to a point about twenty feet out, and merging with everything around me. The difference between myself and the surrounding area, including the other people, lost distinction and difference, and I continued to expand further out at an immediate rate equally in all directions everywhere. Distance was overcome, as if it were all part of my own body.

Fully conscious throughout the entire episode, I felt an enormous shock going from the transition of usual everyday relativity to the boundless; from one extreme to the other within the space of seconds. The experience was not registered in the usual way through the limitation and confinements of the brain and five senses. Rather, I felt the larger area as my subjective self, just as it feels usually within the operation of the individual body. Just as all parts of my body—lung, brain, head, hand, heart—go into making up my entire body, the same was happening on a larger scale. All parts of everything around me—people, furniture, the room—were now part of my being.

But, just as we do not identify with every single aspect of our body, I did not identify with any one particular object or individuality during the expansion of my subjectivity into the Universal Consciousness everywhere. It all felt one and the same. Not knowing how far I was going to go out into everything, or even whether I would return to my individuality, for that matter, I was becoming a little scared. At that point I (my individual ego) called myself back in fear of the unknown. Although I had lost myself relatively at this point, I was still able to call to myself from in my mind: "Come back! Come back!" And in that asking, I did so without any conscious effort on my part. (If there is one thing that ego cannot contend with, it is losing its boundaries of definition and distinction.) Coming back to myself, I noticed a gym member nearby, leaning next to a training machine, asking me with a friendly smile, "Hey, you okay?" Turning to him, I replied, "Yeah." I then simply continued with my next repetition of exercise, as if nothing had happened. The experience was very brief, yet immeasurably intense, having lasted only about five to ten seconds.

Afterward, I returned to my usual, everyday relative/dualistic individual nature with no side effects, except for that of extreme awe, wonder, and curiosity. Never before in my life had I ever experienced such a thing. Because it was so alien to my experience, at the time I thought I was having a heart attack. This was my first encounter of my subjective being becoming boundless and merging back into the Source of all reality in total. My experience also confirmed very directly for me what my doctor and I had been discussing all along, and certainly answered the initial question that had begun my spiritual journey in the first place. The answer I perceived was that the brain merely houses (focuses) consciousness for individual use and operation—that consciousness itself is subjective to all manifest (objective) reality, even to the brain's neurological functions and operation. All reality is in fact a product-expression of consciousness.

I explain my experience by using the classic analogy of the individual wave merging back into the ocean.

You may be thinking that the gym, of all places, is a very strange place to encounter God, and I know there are many spiritual seekers who believe that you can receive mystical union only in the appropriate places, such as the natural environment—in a rain forest, or on a mountain top. These locations certainly set the mood for allowing the Divine to come upon us, but as God is everywhere, there is no location of preference where mystical union is to be experienced. I do feel that it was my immense love for God at the time that allowed grace to do its work and for God to come upon me in such an unorthodox situation, one that was very much appropriate to my situation and lifestyle at the time.

I was twenty-three when I encountered this initial mystical experience, and it has forever changed my orientation to life. Ever since that time, I have developed an undying passion to encounter anything authentically transpersonal, and to share such sacred knowledge and wisdom for the benefit of others. If it were not for this genuine encounter with the mystical, I do not believe I would have had the insight to experience *full* recovery from the illness, which relapsed a further three times later in my twenties. Yes, I had the aid of medication to assist in recovery, but such gross, biochemical material played only a very small role. If it had not been for my own overpowering will and desire to get better, I would never have reclaimed my original identity and well-being again. I would have been just a stunned mullet with chemical reactions, trying to rebalance my brain chemistry. Coming into contact with the subjective nature of reality has allowed me the flexibility to ground my attention in that field and step back from the mind and simply observe the fleeting nature of not only my mind but all aspects of manifest (objective) reality—the emotions, the body, and the exterior environment around me. Now today, four years since my last episode, I have no traces of relapse of the illness whatsoever, and in myself I am just as healthy and "normal" as I was before the illness ever came upon me. To this day, I have yet to come across someone who has recovered to the full extent I have and, in addition, has gone on to realize and experience firsthand the ultimate nature of reality. There may be such people, but I have not encountered them. Yet, having said that, I cannot guarantee that I will never have another relapse. With everything that I have gained from my ten years of experience —both mentally and spiritually—I now have substantial tools and armor to prevent a relapse, and I will do everything in my power to continue to do so.

For those who still may be questioning the authenticity of my mystical experience, I would like to let you know that it occurred quite naturally during normal daily life. I was in good health, and it was not a result of the symptoms of the schizophrenia, such as hallucinations, delusions, grandiose religious identifications (known as The Jesus Syndrome), or special, narcissistic importance. As improbable as this experience may appear, I have two very competent and reliable doctors who specialize in such unique cases as mine and can vouch for my authenticity and credibility.

Since my recovery from the illness, and in the aftermath of my very revealing experience with a nondual state, I now have far greater insight into the subtle aspects of mind and consciousness. Following my own curiosity, I have read much literature in this area of psychology. Reading has only confirmed that which I knew to be true all along, even when I was sick: that we are not the illness we suffer from. What we are, most importantly—beyond our personality and individuality (ego)—is that which is the same in all of us. We are all the same in essence: we are all Human Beings. And our primary nature and essence is never, in any way, separate from the Source of all Life.

No matter what illness we encounter in life—whether mental, emotional, or physical—it can in no way damage or corrupt our deeper subjective self, or ultimately deprive us of experiencing and realizing that greater true aspect of ourself, and reality in total.

From my encounter with the Greater Consciousness, I have found that a true mystical experience is nonprejudicial and nonpreferential, and open and available to anyone, regardless of illness, disability, race, age, gender, sexuality, intelligence, education, qualifications, experience, position, status, wealth, recognition, refinement, realization— and even religious preference, for that matter.

As commonly as spiritual and religious delusion is associated with mental illness, this does not in any way take away from the ultimate reality that even the hell of schizophrenia cannot deprive us of our spiritual essence and source, which is always there—true, pure and free—behind and beyond all the fleeting turmoil observed and experienced at the level of mind. Nor does it take away from the full possibility of a person with mental illness to be just as much open to encounter a genuine authentic spiritual or mystic experience as anyone else may. It may be harder to authenticate given the circumstances, but no less possible.

After my initial "teaser experience" with God, as I like to call it, I was then prepared to encounter the "Big One" awaiting me a few months later in mid-April of 1996, just before Easter. It was a very, very dark night of the soul experience. At the time, my awareness was becoming full of love for God, due to my energy, closeness, and realization of the great reality opening up to me. During a film shoot on Bayview Golf Course on the Northern Beaches of Sydney, Australia, I was working with a film crew of three men and another actor as my counterpart. About midday, with not a cloud in the sky, I had a very emotional reaction to the situation around me. Overwhelmed by the feeling, I collapsed flat on my back in total surrender with my arms stretched out, as if I had been overpowered by some supernatural force coming upon me. In that moment, I felt totally, completely naked, and suddenly my life experience, and all my human ignorance, was being recalled and accounted for upon my human awareness. It was so horrible and felt terrible, because as I lay there it felt as if all my hidden, dark self were being involuntarily released out into the open light of day. I was hurting deeply, and I had absolutely no conscious control over the ordeal—I just had to go with it. It made me feel very naked and exposed to everything, and I was feeling terrible shame, and guilt on my conscience. Once that level of the recall had passed, I then felt the total reverse: the ignorance of humanity and its impact on my individual being. This was truly horrific and the most intense agony I have ever felt in all my life. (I guess God wanted to show me a bit of perspective there, to show me that I am not the only one.)

Once that was finished, I then began to recall all the lives of everyone with and before mine. I was not just witnessing them, I *was* them—

everyone, good and bad. My subjectivity had merged with the collective consciousness of everyone, and I was feeling it all, right back to the beginning of time. It was extremely agonizing, because I was mostly bombarded and impacted by the suffering and ignorance of humanity in totality. There was nothing wrong with the good and harmonious—that was not bothering me—but the darker side of nature did cause me terrible distress and agony. The recall of all life I experienced then was not an ethereal visualization as is usually described in such spiritual phenomena. Rather I *felt* it all upon my being. There was no interior visual association with the recall experience, and I believe it was so intense because of the short time it took to recall it all collectively at that time.

Once I had reached the beginning of time, I then felt the karma of future actions to be due to our actions now. This was rather peculiar: although I could *feel* the result of the future actions, I had no idea what that was, for it had not arrived in the window of the present yet, but it felt just as painful as the rest. The agony experience came to an end with my awareness *feeling* the entire play of creation in totality, the good, the bad, the mixed, past, present, future, all in One—cover to cover. It was at this absolute point that I then came back to the relativity of my bodily senses to notice myself traumatically trying to get up from the fairway on the golf course. (I've always wondered how long I was lying there during the episode.) For the rest of the afternoon I tried to recover from the terrible agony and anguish, which I was still experiencing there before the three men and my fellow actor. No matter how hard I tried, it just would not go away.

About an hour or so later, I was suddenly and instantly engulfed— from completely out of nowhere—by a most beautiful, blissful sensation that I can only describe as feeling like an enormous wave of pure love, so potent and powerful that it completely saturated my entire being. Within the limits of my body, it made me feel completely open and exposed. But now I had nothing to hide, nothing to be ashamed of or guilty about. The feeling and quality of the experience were full of Absolute Truth for me (as clear for all eternity to witness), and I felt totally clean, fresh and free—free from any judgment whatsoever. It felt like pure unconditional love. The love made everything so clean and clear that it felt as if I were merged with the Truth. In the moment of feeling That, both Truth and Love were *felt* to be exactly the same quality, as if the two were One, and I remember standing there in awe, with a still, perplexed look on my face, trying to make some sort of sense of the immense profundity of the feeling that was upon me there and then. Although I was totally exposed in that moment, I felt complete comfort and acceptance by a presence far greater than anything imaginable. (I felt as Adam and Eve must have, before they ate from the tree of knowledge and became ashamed of their nakedness. I felt as if I had stripped the ego veil that covers our souls—the one that was the cause of separation from everything and everyone, including God.) The love I was feeling there and then was far greater than any expressed love I have ever experienced in my life. The moment lasted for only about ten seconds, and then it was gone.

A couple of weeks later, when I had fully recovered from the aftermath of this very intense dark (and light) night of the soul, I felt that an immense cleansing and purification had taken place. As much as I think the term may sometimes be misrepresented or misunderstood in a religious way, I literally *felt* reborn.

A year or so later, after much contemplation, I finally decided to document my extraordinary encounters with the Divine in an autobiographical screenplay trilogy, called *Will Power*. It portrays the hero overcoming the illness (the dark side of nature), his spiritual journey, and his realization of the ultimate nature of reality, which finally leads him to experience universality as the climatic high note to end the trilogy.

Regarding my experience of agony, I also began to deeply appreciate and empathize with what was written in the scriptures about Jesus of Nazareth during the time of his Passion. Around this time I received an insight and wrote it down as a short passage:

Take a moment to contemplate the pains you have encountered on your travels so far.

Then add to that the pains you have yet to encounter till the end of this current life of yours.

Then add to that the same for all the lives that are present, currently.

Then add to that the same for all the lives that have gone before yours.

Then add to that the same for all the lives that will be after yours, currently.

And if then your mind can possibly or even remotely fathom such a unified degree of

pain and suffering, you will know what Christ Jesus felt in His Agony in the Garden.

Thus was His Passion for humanity.

Having come into contact with the Divine has made me believe that all religions have their value, and it is not the case that each religion worships its own unique God, but rather that every religion worships the one and same Creator/Divine Ultimate Reality according to how the cultures of those particular faiths have been influenced by the founding sages who encountered the Divine directly, which ultimately led to their following and teachings about That.

No matter what our degree of perception/awareness may be— whether delusional, accurate, or refined—it does not change the ultimate fact that we all exist in the *same* reality, being on the *same* planet and in the *same* universe. As such, it only seems complementary and natural to me that there is only One Divine Absolute Reality governing it all, no matter where we are located or what path on the map we use to navigate our way back to the Ultimate Treasure of all Life. As a young mystic I would love to see all religions united in a universal spiritual understanding and appreciation that we all exist (and share) in the *same* reality, no matter what path on the map we choose to discover and to use to reach the goal of salvation. As long as we are going in the right direction, and we follow the paths (the faiths) accurately—*free from manipulation and extremism*—we are on the right track!

With absolute respect to all the faiths, Jesus of Nazareth will remain my favorite mystic-sage of all the traditions. However, I would like to look into the spiritual faith of Judaism more, particularly the pure mystical texts and scriptures of the faith.

To close I would like to leave you with a passage of mine to reflect upon: In the realm of the Absolute, everything is subjective.

The Search for Narrative

Mariah Neuroth

I HAVE A PLACE OF MY CHILDHOOD, a place of stillness where I go to be with Jesus. When I close my eyes my feet can feel the water of a river and my legs the slats of wood on the dock. I go here to sit and breathe and be. It is here that I am met by Jesus—not the booming grandeur of the Son of God, but the quiet presence of the Jesus next to me holding my hand. When we are here together we seldom talk ... just lean ever so slightly on each other's shoulders to feel the breeze together. Here he is my companion. We never judge the day or the weather or the time or the dock, just kick the water with our feet and think about the in-betweens of our toes. We go there to be with each other. Just to be with the other.

There has never been a time there with Jesus when I needed to ask questions or pick his brain. In this moment, sitting next to one of history's greatest faith heroes, I witness the Ramadan tradition of giving the best of your meal to someone of another faith, I feel Hanuman enter the world as service and humility, I soar with the Native American's bald eagle as it circles above to signify the realignment of the universe ... and I never need to ask. In this moment I have the answers already; I am aware of myself as faith hero. This awareness nurtures my understanding of Christianity and my role within it. This communion with Christ reconciles my doubts about Christianity and solidifies my commitment to social justice. This story prompts me to take notice of how and where I can invite others to join me on the dock.

I have struggled all my life with many of the details of the Christian tradition. I have often wondered if I was a Christian only because of lineage or if I was a Christian because of Christ. My own experience of Christianity has been unconventional, to say the least. I have touched the boundaries of far left and far right as well as far west and far east. I have found myself frustrated with a liberal Episcopal church more active in politics than spiritual study, a Church of Christ convinced of my damnation after I revealed my desire to be a priest, a Methodist congregation too consumed with material things, and an ashram too distant from my experience of religious tradition.

With each new boundary I reached, I started out toward the other side, longing to know its secrets too. But I always remembered the journey. The limits of my Christian tradition became less and less important to me and the narrative of my journey began to form itself in my mind, creating my own sacred text. This story of my dock re-created my own image of communion with God and gave me the answer to the question of my own Christian legitimacy.

Each piece of this story holds a lesson about my role in the world— a lesson about the inevitable wheres and hows of my life and my inspiration, but one that is driven and derived from that greater WHY. The space, an old wooden dock, holds teachings around both how and where I find my faith. This dock is mine; it comes from my childhood, from a narrative that is indeed written in my lineage. I have nurtured this dock into a safe space where I can find God in the silence, a safe space where my lineage and my Savior can coexist.

This search for narrative began with my first faith hero, my grandfather. He was the Church World Service representative to India in the mid-1960s. He worked with Tibetan refugees, coordinating the powdered milk program, the immunization program, and flood and famine relief. In Vietnam during the war he coordinated the Mennonite Central Committee's war relief effort. In the 1970s he worked in the Philippines, helping indigenous ministers retain their cultural heritage in worship services, and he spent the rest of his life as chaplain to foreign students at Emory University. He died the year I graduated from high school. While I was focusing on the details of his life I realized that none of those details were very relevant to my understanding of who he was and what role he played in my own story. All of those facts and dates came from my research into his life after he passed. While he was alive I knew vaguely who he was politically and academically, and about his works in the world but part of me has always been stirred and awakened by the WHY of him. This is what I inherited. It is the presence of social justice and the spirit of my faith tradition, the why of my work in the world. This was the first chapter of my narrative.

Inspired by the life of my grandfather, I have had the honor of dedicating myself to the work of faith and social justice. The narrative that my grandfather left for me also inspired me to understand and identify my own faith and the narrative that this faith provides. I have found myself at times getting caught up in the day-to-day HOW of my work and longing to connect to the greater WHY that motivates me each day—the same WHY of my grandfather that stirred me so deeply. The faith heroes and great leaders whom I admire were calling me into a deeper relationship with them, into an even deeper understanding of my role in the world and the faith that brings me to it—and all of this through my own narrative, my own story of faith. I began to wonder if I could share the dock with these faith heroes too.

My grandfather always said he was in the world but not of the world. To a seventeen-year-old kid this sounded like the words of her senile old grandfather, but to this twenty-four-year-old woman, that is what now shapes my life. There is a part of my family history, the legacy left for me that lives, recreates itself daily in my mind. This history lives in that narrative that I have been writing inside myself from a very young age. Some of this legacy is fiction, made up from a child's imagination. Some of this narrative is true, brought to life by storytellers and late nights on the river with my family reliving their adventures.

Storytelling has been a significant part of my life and my relationships. There is a common connection through story. Our faith traditions teach through them, our families pass down their heritage through them, and our minds and hearts identify through the narrative that these stories provide. This verbal masala became the text of my faith tradition. Chapters of the Bible followed by Rumi's words and the wisdom of the Tao Te Ching are all pieces of the narrative that identifies me. This narrative that I sought and continue to seek lies in the lives of my faith heroes, a group that has grown to be more inclusive for me. My own understanding of and communion with Jesus led me to the teachings of other great faith heroes, to relationships with other faith heroes and ultimately into a deeper understanding of myself as a Christian. My meditations, guided by the Taoist tradition, focused on Christ. My image of Jesus was solidified by my understanding of the Taoists' nonbeing. I recognized the image of my Savior in the words of the Taoist's holy text. And my relationship to this image of Jesus, of my grandfather, of myself is where I found my place in a faith tradition, in a community of religiously diverse friends and in a career of social justice.

The teachings of Lao Tzu and the Taoist tradition have taught me to connect with my own presence. Without this understanding I could have never experienced communion with the heroes that carved faith into my heart.

> The mind is desperate to fix the river in place: Possessed by the ideas of the past, preoccupied with the images of the future, it overlooks the plain truth of the moment. The one who can dissolve her mind will suddenly discover the Tao at her feet, and clarity at hand.
>
> Hua Hu Ching 21

I have felt those moments when the distractions of the day and the overwhelming reality of our world have dissolved into the present moment and birthed connection and communion in its essence. I have discovered the Tao at my feet, soaking in the river next to Christ, sharing space with my Savior.

There is a thread in my narrative that continues to guide me. It is the same stirring that I felt for my grandfather and my Savior, the WHY of them in the world. My colleagues at the Interfaith Youth Core describe a stirring when they read their own sacred texts, regardless of tradition. When I watch youth from all different religious backgrounds read their own sacred texts, they can describe this stirring. What I have realized is that I am similarly stirred by the narrative of my faith tradition, the text that has been written by the lives of my faith heroes. I describe the interfaith work that I do now as a coming together around the table of stirring. Coming together, stirred by vastly different texts but stirred nonetheless, coming together to a common faith, bringing the individual connections that we may have for our particular faith traditions and recognizing the common faith that this stirring creates. The commonality of faith—a faith that invites each one to dip his or her feet into that river of answers and presence—invites every faith hero to be a companion on the dock and to share in the creation of a narrative. In this we can lean ever so slightly on one another's shoulders to feel the breeze together. We do not judge the day or the weather, the time or the space. In this faith we are simply present, holding hands and thinking about the in-betweens of our toes.

The Fly Box

DAN JOHNSON

1. Fly-fishing: fishing with a long pole and a long line (with a "fly" attached to the end), which is gradually cast into the water a few feet at a time as the pole is waved over the head. A fly is an artificial fish lure, sometimes made by hand, which looks like one of many kinds of river flies. Some flies are very beautiful.
2. Creative interaction: the process by which we make friends and develop our personalities. The first step is to be open and trusting with another person. Mutual appreciation occurs as we incorporate parts of our personalities. Over time, we are transformed.

SCENE 1

(A historic house, Grinnell, Iowa, USA, winter of 2003.)

I am at an event organized by the Iowa Peace Institute to honor three young people, from three countries, who are traveling around the world speaking for peace. The dining room has a big table full of beautiful food.

Glenn Leggett, aged 85, retired president of Grinnell College, sitting in a comfortable chair in the corner, has the appearance of a happily aging king. With a smile on his face, cane in hand, immaculately groomed (as always), a charismatic good spirit, he is confidently holding court.

I'm getting food at the buffet table.

GLENN: Hello.

DAN: Why aren't you out fishin' on this beautiful day?

GLENN: No fish today (smiles).

DAN: Someday I'm going fly-fishing.

GLENN: Oh?

DAN: Yeah.

GLENN: Have you got equipment?

DAN: Yeah, my dad's.

GLENN: Oh, what's that?

DAN: Well, when my father died he gave me a fly rod, a reel, and a little box five inches around and one inch deep, with a cloudy plastic top and a "trick" release button.

(Fifteen years after my father's death, on the weathered wooden porch of a big old house, overlooking a pond in the woods, I had struggled to open this box for the first time. The sun came out. I relaxed and pushed on the little silver button on top of the box. It moved. I pushed down and tried to lift the top off. No luck. I pushed down again and turned the top to the left. A small pie-shaped compartment opened. It contained several little, brilliantly colored hand-tied flies. I kept turning the top to discover more flies, and at that moment, I felt my father's presence.)

Glenn looks in my eyes, smiles and nods. Then we eat and talk to other people.

SCENE II

A couple of weeks later, Glenn calls.

GLENN: Do you want to see my fly-fishing equipment?

DAN: Oh yeah, that'd be great.

GLENN: Okay, come over tomorrow afternoon.

DAN: Okay, see ya then.

The next day I go to Glenn's beautiful home a few blocks from my home. His wife, Russelle, meets me at the door. Glenn soon appears and we slowly make our way downstairs to his basement, which is full of fishing equipment and a computer workspace.

Glenn shows me his fly rods and how to use them. Then, surprisingly, he gives me a rod, a reel, and a book on fly-fishing. He invites me to go fishing with him "as soon as the fish are biting." But first, he says, we need to practice casting on a pond in the country. I go home and start to read the book.

SCENE III

A few weeks later my wife, Debbie, and I invite Glenn and Russelle to dinner at our home. Glenn brings more gifts; leaders, strike indicators, information about different kinds of trout, and a little rectangular box, four inches by six inches, one inch deep, with a clear plastic top, containing about twenty-five flies he has tied (including a handwritten description of each fly). He tells me how to use all this stuff, and we talk about going to the pond to practice casting. I show him my dad's flies and rods, which he admires lavishly.

A few days later we get a letter from Glenn thanking us for the excellent dinner, showering us with compliments, and inviting me to get ready to go fishing in the springtime.

SCENE IV

Then Glenn calls.

GLENN: Want to practice your casting?
DAN: Yes.
GLENN: Come on over.
DAN: Okay.

I take a beautiful rug made by Tibetan refugees.

GLENN: Are you sure you want to give us this?

DAN: Oh, yes. I've been to the place where they're made, and I want you to have this one.

It's a cool, windy day in March. We spend a half hour in the field behind his home casting downwind, sidewind, and upwind. I've read the book he gave me, and I ask about casting and "mending the line."

GLENN: Do what feels right. Enjoy yourself. Relax. Take time to look around and get in touch with nature. If other people are with you, enjoy them. If you're by yourself, it's a good time to be alone.

Glenn has a strong personality but lots of humility. Here he is, in his eighty-fifth year, teaching me (me?) how to fly-fish, how to appreciate nature, how to take time and give something of lasting value to another person, even when he is so aware that his life is short and precious. He makes me feel like a friend rather than a student. We share some stories and ideas. We creatively interact in such a way that I feel an expanded awareness of reality that enriches me and is the beginning of another personal transformation.

This relationship deepens my appreciation for other people and helps me understand the connections we all have with each other.

Wow! Let's go fishing. Yes!

FINAL ACT

I never see or speak to Glenn again. He goes to a big hospital for two weeks. When he comes home to a small local retirement place he has an infection, so except for a few people, visitors are not allowed.

I have just read a new book, *The Tibetan Book of Living and Dying*, so I try to do some of the things suggested for relating to a dying person. Over several days, I send a funny card, then a drawing I made of a fly fisherman, then a picture of ducks landing on a pond, then a big bouquet of flowers. I want to sit next to Glenn, be a good listener, share some jokes, help him take care of business, help him die peacefully. He doesn't need help. He has plenty of help. I need it. I feel powerless and hopeless, and that is the point at which many people turn to their faith for help.

Then I realize something. Some of Glenn's generous, insightful personality is now part of my personality, and this exceptionally good feeling replaces the feelings of denial, grief, and loss that I have when he dies.

We haven't quite made it to the pond to practice casting or to the trout stream to catch fish in the springtime, but I know that when I open Glenn's fly box, I will feel his presence. I feel it now.

How the AIDS Pandemic Changed My Life

MA JAYA SATI BHAGAVATI

I HAVE OFTEN BEEN ASKED what pivotal moments have changed my life and what has deepened my heart. Many of us strive to have a deeper awareness and to be present for humanity. I believe there are no throwaway people. One of the most important things I have learned is that if we change just one small thing there is an opportunity to create a shift in the world. Let us remember that just a simple smile can soothe someone's heart and create change.

I have been working with life and death since the beginning of AIDS.

Many years ago, on a day cooler than usual for Los Angeles, the hospitals were filled to capacity. It was the early 1990s. We were on our way to a hospital in West Hollywood to see a young man who had heard about a group of people visiting people with AIDS. He didn't want to see me or any of my students for fear that we would be appalled at the condition of his body. As we entered his room in the AIDS ward, I thought my eyes were deceiving me; I had never seen such suffering. His body was covered with the worst case of Kaposi's sarcoma I had ever seen. Without hesitation, I jumped into the bed with him and held him tightly. He began to scream, and then he began to laugh. "Oh Ma," he cried out, "I have not been out of my house for six months. I watched my body shrivel up as the AIDS virus has taken over."

Looking him in his eyes, I said, "Feel it, son; feel it in the depth of your heart and know that you are not this body." He died shortly after our visit, with greater hope in his heart. This experience changed my life forever.

I know in the depth of my heart that the Parliament of the World's Religions can make a difference. This is the forum where we can tell the stories and bring the awareness to everybody's heart that AIDS is not over. It is our responsibility to bring awareness to the issues that plague our globe, to create healing and the possibility of world peace.

I am reminded of my Travis. He was four years old and weighed twelve pounds. When I went to see him, his mouth was filled with sores; the doctors did not have anything to cure his condition. Knowing that this small child would love a sweet treat, I took a straw and begin placing drops of soda in his mouth. His pain began to ease. He had not spoken for many days; he was a mere shadow of his former self. His eyes opened and he looked at me with the knowledge of eternity in his four-year-old withered body. He said two words: "Thank you." I thought my heart would break. Travis enjoyed his little sips of soda. He was never able to speak again, but he would nod and his little fingers would reach to touch my face. His courage changed my life forever. This young boy reminded a grown woman the meaning of two words: *thank you.* I remember wherever I go to share these two words, because gratitude can change our lives and change how we view and serve humanity.

I remember a little girl named Leslie who had multiple sclerosis as well as AIDS; she was one of thousands of young children who had been raped. She did not blame the world. She had so much courage and lived through so much heartache. I think back and remember how I held her as we spoke of death. I watched her smile with her first understanding of the knowledge that she was going to die. She finally understood why she couldn't play or ride a bicycle or run around like other children. I was able to share the Christ of her heart, and she was at peace in that moment. She brought me to my own true being.

So who will hear my story? I think back to a very special day in 1993, when I spoke at the Parliament of the World's Religions in Chicago. I shared sacred poetry and the story of a young girl named Dena who suffered with AIDS. I can still remember the depth of silence in a room filled with thousands of people as I shared my experience of working with people with AIDS.

The Parliament has changed my life and has listened. I feel that we have learned to listen to each other and acknowledge our differences. As hunger, pain, violence, and disease spread throughout this world, I know we will have a voice—a voice that will be heard.

At the 1999 Parliament I walked through the streets of New Rest Township in Cape Town. A young man named Tondo stole my heart. His story was one of pain and suffering. He had lived through the wrath of ignorance and prejudice during the time of apartheid. He suffered so badly and was once left for dead, and yet he picked himself up and found work. He chose not to move out of the township but to help create a future for those who live there. He is raising a young son on his own. He brought us to his home and shared his life, his pain, and his people. We were invited to the town hall and were welcomed by the community leaders. We bought fruit, food, and school supplies for the community. We met the youth of New Rest. We went to the corner where a woman was selling fruit, and we bought her produce. Babies with bellies distended and hungry waited in line at their mother's hips, and we shared a moment offering our gifts of love.

Tondo walked us around the township, heat from the African sky beating down, and he proudly showed us the plans for a school building and future homes. This is a memory that will last me forever. One who speaks of another's life with passion can create change. That day in Cape Town was the beginning of a lasting relationship with the people of New Rest. We undertook the task to help to complete the Creche. Our plans include a marketplace to help people in the community earn a living selling their wares. The Parliament of the World's Religions offers opportunities to expand with the gift of giving to others.

I think of my children in Uganda, seven hundred orphans being taken care of at Ma's Orphan Providence House. It is run by a beautiful Catholic priest, Father Centurio, who has suffered from religious violence and loss. Many children who have AIDS have lost both parents to AIDS and know they are dying—dying from indifference. I met Father Centurio through my interfaith work, at a conference where I begged people to listen that AIDS is not over yet. Here we found each other, and we continue to share our lives as we reach over an ocean of compassion.

I write this story overlooking a body of water on my ashram named after the holy river in India, the Ganga. This body of water holds the ashes of many hundreds and hundreds of our dead, many who have died because of the AIDS virus.

I am honored that people ask for their ashes to have a resting place in our sacred Ganga. Here they have a place to be in death as well as in life.

Since AIDS, my life has changed dramatically. I acknowledge in my own being that the force of God, Goddess, self, Buddha—the force of something deep within—must be used to create peace. I realize that every one of us has so much more to do.

My life changed in the face of AIDS. My life changed in the face of pain and hunger. I pray that we all become more generous—not just with money, but also with our time and our hearts. My religion is the religion of kindness, generosity, and gratitude. One does not have to believe a certain way to feel his or her heart and to feel the hearts of others. Being with the dying has taught me compassion and kindness. I see so much courage that there is no choice but to do more.

Four black folks raised me in the streets under the boardwalk in Coney Island; they were alcoholics, prostitutes, and drug addicts. It was here that I learned the great brightness of being loved that prepared me for the moment I live in now. I take my stories, the moments that have changed my life, and I hold them in my heart. I bring them to paper with two words: *thank you.*

Religious Diversity on the Spiritual Path

Annapurna Astley

I STARTED INTERFAITH WORK when I was three years old. Descended from Scottish Presbyterians, my Unitarian Universalist (UU) parents enrolled me in a preschool at the local synagogue. I was raised with intellectual northerners who were open to different ways of thinking and expression and were not overtly spiritual. The UUs draw mainly from the Judeo-Christian heritage, though one of the nineteenth century's most famous UU ministers, Ralph Waldo Emerson, studied and took to heart the Hindu writings of the Bhagavad Gita. There is an appreciation of ritual and service, tradition and study, community outreach and religious education. In Sunday School we read, discussed, debated, and analyzed the Bible; celebrated Jewish holidays; and learned the symbolism of Eastern traditions. My first visit to a Buddhist community was when I was about thirteen, a field trip of our church's Sunday School. The Barre Center for Buddhist Studies, a Vipassana retreat center, introduced us to sitting and walking meditation and to the concept of a silent retreat directed only by a bell ringing. In fact, I remember that an entire year of Sunday School was spent visiting neighboring churches and religious communities. Our UU church, the second oldest parish in Worcester, Massachusetts, is certainly rooted in the Christian faith, but members participate without signing on to any particular belief or creed. It is up to the UU individual to discover his or her own "personal theology" (www.uu.org), whereas the community's role is to support the individual in this journey. Equipped with a value system that accepted many coexisting responses to the deepest questions of life, I began to understand the weight of the responsibility and freedom of this search. As poet Rainer Maria Rilke might say, I began to "live the questions."

As a teenager I began to study spiritual writings on my own. I read *Handbook to Higher Consciousness* by Ken Keyes Jr., when I was sixteen. Keyes's philosophy combined Christian, Buddhist, and Hindu teachings and gave sound bites for the beginner on the spiritual path. I met a young mystic who led me to an experience of interconnectedness with nature. I gradually stopped eating meat. I started studying and practicing yoga. I constantly questioned the nature of reality and sought to experience it more deeply.

As a freshman at Harvard I explored various introductory humanities courses, such as anthropology and psychology, but was utterly captivated by the study of religion. My first course was Diana Eck's Introduction to World Religions: Diversity and Dialogue. As I was exposed in rigorous academic coursework to the spectrum of belief systems, I continued in my extracurricular time to participate in spiritual study. I became more involved with yoga and meditation classes, and I joined a shamanic practice group at Harvard's Center for the Study of World Religions. Furthermore, my part-time job as an undergraduate was to help with collecting data for the Pluralism Project, Professor Eck's research into religious communities in America. On many levels, I was fascinated by the spiritual experience and its expression by communities around the globe. Some would say I was majoring in religion. I would say religion was majoring in me.

In my sophomore year, I met my guru. I was taking Professor Eck's course Hindu Myth, Image and Pilgrimage in which she announced that a Christian, Jewish Guru who works with people with AIDS was going to be speaking at the Divinity School in an evening lecture.

Fascinated, I showed up. The room was packed as incense burned, and large photos of bedridden patients surrounded the room. Ma Jaya Sati Bhagavati (Ma) entered, immediately declaring, "The accent's Brooklyn!" Ma was all energy, all movement, all passion. She was compassion and humor. She told stories of the dying, of laughing and crying with them in their final days. She would seamlessly shift into a deep and silent meditation, bringing the room to a warm silence. It is impossible to summarize her presence and presentation. It was experiential. I was blown away and curious. She was almost too much for me. But I wanted more. She had devotion. She had no fear. In the midst of a silent meditation, I felt my heart explode.

I met Ma after the second talk she gave at Harvard, and she invited me to her ashram, Kashi, in Florida, to learn more about her work. I took her up on her offer for two weeks in the summer of 1994. Ma's story is truly unique and extraordinary. No one can tell it the way she can, but I will try to summarize it briefly. Ma had forged a way to combine and teach the diverse spiritual lineages of her life and to share her passion for humanity. Born to Jewish parents, and losing her mother at a young age, she spent her young life on Coney Island, befriending the people she calls her first spiritual teachers: four black homeless people under the boardwalk. As a teenager she married a Catholic, and in her thirties she began yoga classes to lose weight. Intense breath-work catalyzed her into a mystical visitation of Jesus Christ, and later she met Swami Nityananda and Baba Neem Karoli, her guru. Nothing in her life experience in that point had introduced her to Hindu philosophy or teachings, and her life rapidly changed. Over the past thirty years, she has continued to teach and share her experiences. In 1976 she founded Kashi Ashram, an interfaith spiritual community rooted in her teachings, in Sebastian, Florida.

Over the past nine and one-half years I have continued to study with Ma, and for nearly six years I have lived at Kashi Ashram. I would say that Ma's basic philosophy does not conflict with that with which I was raised. In both there is a strong emphasis on service to humanity and celebration of a variety of spiritual paths. A similar value is placed on spiritual community, traditions, and rituals. The main cultural difference, I would say, is the additional expression of Hindu ritual in her community. The vocabulary on the ashram is what I call "Ma's Brooklynese Sanskrit." *Puja* is moving prayer, sometimes at the *dhunis* (fire hearths), sometimes at the temples and shrines; *darshan* is when we see Ma in a community (*satsang*) setting; the spiritual names she gives her students, such as my own, Annapurna, are usually (though not always) names of Hindu deities or aspects of the Divine. The Hindu concept of the guru, or spiritual teacher, was new to me as well. It took a little time to adjust to living in such a large community and its energy, but the essence of Kashi has never felt foreign to me; on the contrary, it has always felt like home.

The Kashi community has offered opportunities to engage with the worldwide interfaith movement. Since 1994, Ma has been a trustee of the Council for the Parliament of the World's Religions, an interfaith organization headquartered in Chicago. The CPWR organizes large conferences every five years. For the 1999 Parliament in Cape Town, South Africa, Kashi organized a delegation of which I was a part. As a young adult, I applied and was accepted into the Next Generation Assembly Team, a group of youth from around the world and from various traditions. It was the most intensive interfaith team-building experience I had ever been involved with. Led by passionate and sensitive facilitators, such as Patrice Brodeur, Josh Borkin, and Eboo Patel, this group of thirty-five young people produced a presentation in six days that rocked the Parliament to its core. In a simple and profound way, we introduced ourselves to the Assembly of Religious Leaders and stated our commitments to changing our corners of the world. We formed a circle around the leaders at their tables and passed the wireless mike, speaking one at a time—Muslim, Sikh, Christian, Jew, Hindu, Native African, on and on. We expressed commitments to small changes, or to continuing what was already begun: mentoring, praying, working in the arts, becoming better on our own paths, sharing what we had experienced in Cape Town. That circle remains for me a circle of solidarity and interfaith prayer and support for everything that I do. Knowing that my peers and friends, all over the world, are back in their home countries continuing in their work is sometimes enough to keep me going through the challenges of this work.

The following story illustrates a moment in my life when my spiritual path was affected by an experience I had in a religious setting that was new to me. I was a guest in a black Pentecostal church, not far from the ashram where I live. A co-worker, Lisa, at an arts summer camp whom I had known and worked with for two years had invited me. I had a healthy respect for Lisa and her work with children; trusted and admired her style of love, protection, and enjoyment of the campers. Lisa and I had set up the visit ahead of time, and, as it turned out, the visit coincided with the first Sunday after September 11, 2001. I had been feeling shattered by the events that had occurred. The sense of trauma, tragedy, and fear, as well as the media images, had not stopped. The moment I entered Lisa's church, I was lovingly embraced and welcomed along with the friends from the ashram who had come with me. The only white (including one Jewish) folks in the small church, we were warmly encouraged to participate and share in the service. For the first time since the shocking events had occurred, I felt a deep sense of peace and safety. Why? The congregants voiced a strong faith, which held them in a place that lacked any fear. The sermon that day taught me: "Why fear? We have God when we are alive; we have God when we are dead." I realized that terrorism can make you afraid only if you let it. The faith and wisdom of a people terrorized for centuries had brought them beyond fear, and this small congregation in the deep South, far from the large northern cities, was not allowing itself to be terrorized. I was very grateful for the lessons I received that day from my neighbors and from our common divine source.

The opportunity to share my perceptions and stories in this forum of young interfaith travelers has urged me to continue asking two related questions: (1) Who is "the other?" and (2) in the words of the mantra of Hindu sage Ramana Maharshi, "Who am I?" I wonder: Where does the delineation occur between "me" and "another"? Who draws the line? What makes one neighbor "different" from me and another "the same"? Contemporary Zen teacher Roshi Bernie Glassman draws from a rich Buddhist tradition that challenges the same issue. When asked in an interview, "What's the source of the ... profound commitment that you have to alleviate the suffering of others?" he responded, "I don't see them as others. It's pretty egocentric. I want to have less suffering!" (*What Is Enlightenment?* Magazine interview by Andrew Cohen, www.wie.org).

Glassman's reality includes such interdependence between beings that he sees all suffering as his own—and shared. Ramana Maharshi and Glassman touch on a view echoed in many of the world's traditions: that duality and separation are misperceptions, and that spiritually is only interconnected oneness. Emerson calls it the Oversoul. While this teaching resonates with me spiritually, nonetheless I feel that in the realm of interfaith work we need to celebrate and respect different perceptions and expressions of truth. As a child I was influenced by the appreciation of multiple forms of worship, and as an adult I continue to learn each time I am introduced to a new worldview.

Sacred Story

AQUIL CHARLTON

HEARING THE BELIEFS OF OTHERS helps tune our ears to the sound of God being evoked in our presence. We can listen to the plights of others for familiar stepping stones and stumbling blocks that remind us of our own path. We are all just trying to reach God. We can clarify our missions and confirm our beliefs in circles of people that include the religious "other." I have engaged in interfaith work because I want to find a common language through which I may talk to others about God.

I believe that grammar school Christmas parties and South Side playgrounds should be the testing grounds for the development of this interfaith language. I believe this because the development of a religious identity begins for many people as early as their baptism, briss, or *shehada*. However, in our youth we rarely have the capacity to understand what that means when it comes to our relationships with people of backgrounds, beliefs, and experiences that are different from ours. Encounters with the cultural or religious "other" happen frequently for children in Chicago's public schools and neighborhoods—at least they did for me.

My formal engagement in interfaith work was with a group of eight high school students, called the Chicago Youth Council, through the Interfaith Youth Core. During the spring of 2003, I helped lead the youth through the completion of the Sacred Stories Project, for which they composed written works describing their perspectives on how each of their religious traditions encourage the value of hospitality. Each student transformed her or his written work into a spoken-word piece, all of which were recorded and compiled onto an audio CD. The students encouraged me to write a piece for the project as well, which I will share to explain some of my own story. The following piece describes some of the learning experiences that have helped me shape the way I share my relationship with God with my fellow humans.

The first meaningful experience occurred during interreligious discussions with my South Side Little League teammates over sienna-colored dirt and cans of Nehi soda. It was the Jets, last game of the season, but the most important thing to us that day was reaching consensus about Jesus. They groaned like old folks as words like "prophet" failed me when I tried to explain what it was that I thought Muslims believe, and I stumbled upon words like "mortal" and "died." My teammates believed in Jesus's resurrection. I did not, and none of us could explain why, except for "Well, my momma said ..." Black and white batting gloves spelled out our frustration in sharp hand gestures, expressing the severity of our need to reach a common understanding. And our attempts fell at our speckled cleats through clouds of cinnamon-colored dust. I wish I had known then that the Qur'an alludes to Jesus's resurrection. I wish I had known then how to communicate to my teammates that the most important thing to me is the immortal example that the Prophet Jesus, peace be upon him, provided for us. I believe they would have agreed. Instead, for the rest of the game they shook their heads in disdain every time I swung and missed, whispering to each other, "That's because he doesn't believe in Jesus," missing the point completely.

Later on, in the third grade, another learning experience occurred, during long explanations of why I did not dress up for Halloween and why I was not going be anyone's "Secret Santa" or exchange gifts at the class Christmas party. This was before teachers called them holiday parties. At these parties I usually ended up bursting my classmates' Santa Claus bubbles, sending all of them home to interrogate their parents—except for Vicky. Her parents are Hindu.

I learned more while questioning cafeteria caterers about the contents of their concessions and reading the backs of food wrappings for the lists of ingredients. I learned that Twinkies are made with animal shortening, which probably comes from pigs, and that Salisbury steak at school lunch was probably not beef (or anything else raised on a farm, for all that we knew). I ate a lot of peanut butter and jelly sandwiches as a child; it is still my favorite snack.

I had another experience while listening to my group of campers sing along while David, a balding singer-storyteller, played his guitar. David would jump up and down, the flapping of his sandals on the concrete courtyard adding percussion to songs about peace, togetherness, and the observance of Shabbat, the Jewish Sabbath. During my employment as a counselor at the Hyde Park Jewish Community Center's summer day camp, I first learned about the importance of community in the celebration of religious holy days. I spent five days out of the week in this religious community for seven summers in a row—more time than I had spent with any religious community at that point in my life. I was raised in a Muslim household, yet I learned how to sing the *motzi* and bless the challah, wine, and candles for Shabbat in Hebrew before I knew how to properly perform *Wudu* for my five daily prayers or say them in Arabic.

Another important event happened during the holy month of Ramadan, while I ignored my classmates as they slowly and deliberately ate french fries in front of me. I attempted to explain to them that fasting is not intended to be a hardship on any Muslim and that I had eaten a big breakfast before the sun rose, which, God willing, would sustain me until I returned home in the evening to break the fast. My nephew, Tariq, was ten years old when he said to me, "I know that the fast is supposed to help me strengthen my faith, so when my friends tease me I know it is Allah reminding me of why I fast." He articulated then what I could not when I was fourteen. I quoted him for an article on Ramadan I wrote for my school's newspaper, and that was all the more important to me.

I learned even more when my friends encouraged me to question my faith and my brother, Na'eem, directed me to the Qur'an so that I might find some answers. My mother gave me the only copy of the Qur'an that I own. My brother gave me some ideas about where to start reading. Na'eem practiced fatherhood in our father's absence. The first time I entered a mosque it was with Na'eem. The imam was a black man. I listened. He reminded me of my brother, to whom I listen more than he knows.

Another shocking experience was transformed into spiritual learning when I was robbed at gunpoint for the third time. The only words in my head were *"Le-illehe-il-allah, le-illehe-il-allah, le-illehe-il-allah!"* This is because Na'eem told me that if these are the last words I utter before I die, I will be forgiven of all my sins and will enter paradise for eternity.

And, when I was discussing with my girlfriend, Chakka, the hopes we have for raising children together, that flash of learning happened again. She wants our children to be humble and to respect and appreciate their parents. She hopes that they will believe in a power outside themselves that will call them to their highest being, from which they will be filled with the motivation to practice hospitality and social responsibility. We agreed that we are excellent role models, and that our religious communities and practices have a great deal to do with that. We want our children to have strong values. We have faith that both the Baptist church and the mosque are places where good values are taught. We have faith in our abilities and the abilities of our families to direct our children toward finding their own paths to God, to respect the paths that the people around them have found, and to trust their parents' guidance. To me it was a miracle that Chakka and I focused on our shared values throughout our conversation about our future together. I can honestly thank Eboo, April, Kiley, and the mission and scope of the Interfaith Youth Core for helping me find the words to express to the love of my life the faith I have that we are on the right path.

Another life-changing realization occurred as I was listening to Imam A. Malik Mujahid, from Sound Vision, deliver the *Kudbah* at the Downtown Islamic Center for Jumah the Friday after the official beginning of our nation's war with Iraq. We had talked while walking to the mosque from an interfaith vigil for all victims of war. He asked for my help with recruiting our Muslim brothers as volunteers for the seventy-two-hour vigil. His desire for peace among the peoples of the earth moved him to tears. His heartfelt address inspired at least ten brothers to volunteer for the vigil between seven o'clock that evening and seven the next day.

Two weeks ago, I sat with my eyes closed listening to Aisha sing the *Adhan*, the call to prayer, in Arabic. Again I experienced that feeling of revelation as I sat with my eyes closed, smiling wide while Sam and Adins sang songs together in Hebrew; as I sat with my eyes closed, hearing Diana speak in her native Spanish for the first time; as I sat with my eyes closed, absorbed in the imagery that Amin was able to create with perfect pace and inflection; as I sat with my eyes closed, feeling the energy, like fire, from the recording booth as Yusra implored her community and the leaders of our nations to ask themselves if they are doing enough to practice hospitality; as I sat with my eyes closed, listening to the intricate patterns of Christine's retelling of the parable of the Good Samaritan; as I sat with my eyes closed, waiting to hear how Zeeshan decided to conclude his sacred story; as I sat with my eyes closed tight in prayer, thanking Allah for the creativity that Luv n' Dedication brought about in the Chicago Youth Council. I sat with my eyes wide open in amazement at the chemistry between the Chicago Youth Council members, their creativity, and their eloquence.

When I read Surah 49: Al Hujurat, where Allah says, "Oh humankind, We created you from a single pair of male and female, and made you into nations and tribes, that ye may know each other, not that ye may despise each other," it occurred to me that this is the divine design of the earth and its inhabitants.

It occurred to me like revelation.

Vision of the Future

SWAMI SHRADDHANANDA (MAUREEN DOLAN)

F OR THE SECOND TIME IN MY LIFE, I was consciously facing death. The onset of severe flu and the development of pneumonia came fast and fierce in December 1999, right around the time of the last Parliament of the World's Religions. While I did not die physically, a transition in consciousness most assuredly took place, shaking me to the core and opening my heart and life to new possibilities.

Just after my fiftieth birthday and four years into my priesthood, I became so ill that I was rushed to the hospital in subzero weather. I was unable to eat, talk, read, write, or even lie down because breathing was so difficult. I have since learned that many of the 40 to 50 million American women passing through menopause often experience a life-changing illness around the age of fifty.

This was truly a stopping place for me to reevaluate my life and spiritual service. I thought I had been doing good work at a public interest nonprofit law agency, I thought I was doing enough to feed my spirit, but some new regeneration beckoned. Subtler, larger forces were at work to realign people and events on this planet. The illness forced me to just Be. I found I could do nothing but sit, propped up, with IVs running in my veins and oxygen pumping into me. With no interest in TV or other stimulation, I meditated. I meditated for seven days, nearly every moment I was hospitalized.

When I was at my worst, my sister and I discussed facing death and facing life. I told her I felt so very tired (pneumonia and the prescribed medicine both contributed to incredible fatigue), had no regrets, and was losing desire for any experiences at all. I said that maybe my work here was done. Then I said, "Well, maybe I could live for service." She jumped on that and said, "Yes, service is a great reason to keep on living!" Ah, the purposeful life.

There was a full moon on December 21, the Winter Solstice, a special time for those in my spiritual tradition. From the hospital window the lunar light loomed large and wondrous. My meditations had given me deeper experience in the joy of egolessness. To be truly without desires for a sustained period is to feel real freedom. Bliss and wonder.

At this full moon and out of the silence of meditation came three visions. In the first, I saw the creation of a housing cooperative where I was living with others and doing social justice work. In the second, circles upon circles of women spiraled in discussion groups, meditation circles, and interfaith rituals and ceremonies. In the third vision, I was walking into a nebulous but exciting future where I was asked to play a larger role in peacemaking on the planet with many, many others—hundreds of thousands turning into millions, and I was simply one of them.

These visions came as distinct realities, almost like clear memories, and not as figments of my imagination. I knew from past study and experience of yoga and meditation that these visions came through a doorway of subtle universal energies. In my tradition, Swami Yogananda, Shri Yukteshwar, and Goswami Kriyananda had written many works which illustrated the truth of this kind of experience.

I knew from my own experience that these visions were not passing fancies but rather tastes of light, *siddhis*. In the yoga tradition, *siddhis* are known as by-products of intense meditation and clear seeing. In the Celtic tradition, *siddhis* are shared magical powers. The age-old formula (intensity times duration equals force) was at work. I knew from my studies of the new physics, as well as from my study of meditation, that utter freedom gives the possibility of exploring time and space in different ways.

During my stay at the hospital, a Christian minister appeared one day at my door. Because I remained so content in my meditative state, I did not want an interruption. After I said no to having a visit, he asked me three times if my name was really Maureen Dolan, verifying the spelling and pronunciation. I thought that was odd, but then he was gone. Twenty minutes later a middle-aged woman, dressed in simple gray and black, entered. She pulled up a chair to the bedside and asked me to look at her ID badge. It said "Sister Maureen Dolan, Chaplain." We had a good laugh about meeting and talked a bit about Eastern philosophy and also the writings of Teilhard de Chardin. When she left, I knew this synchronicity had given me another lesson in meeting myself more deeply.

After my recovery, my personality changed in subtle ways. I was softer-spoken, more delighted in living in the moment, and more firmly rooted in priestessing on the planet. My meditation practice, my yoga teaching, and my commitment to ministry deepened. A new enthusiasm enveloped my life as I began to bring the visions I had encountered to life in the material plane.

THE FIRST VISION

Within two months of the pneumonia crisis, I initiated a circle of women's cross quarter celebrations (cross quarters—February 1, May 1, August 1, November 1—are those times exactly between the equinoxes and solstices, honored across the planet in many spiritual traditions and commemorated through tens of thousands of years of human history).

This group, which grew to over fifty women, has met four times a year for the past four years. The first vision was realized.

The curiosity I had about my vision of those spiraling women propelled me to study anthropological and historical works. I wanted to understand more deeply the belief systems that predated Christianity, Islam, and Judaism, and other "more modern" religions. The mystery awakened in the vision of those circling women seemed to hark back to ancient times, and I wanted to see what links existed between my own tradition of Kriya yoga and other traditions. While my studies in the seminary had included comparative religion classes, it was time to delve more deeply into the subject. Because the Winter Solstice had marked such a transformation in me, I wanted to understand the significance of astrological dates better.

What I found was that indigenous peoples throughout the world had the stars in common and organized eight major celebrations in the year. From shamans in South America to ancient yogis to adherents of the Celtic tradition to the goddess-centered cultures of Catal Huyuk and other places, the seasons were marked by these dates: solstices (June 21 and December 21), equinoxes (March 21 and September 21), and the cross quarter dates in between those four seasonal markers. I also discovered that many of our present-day holidays, commemorations, and holy days of more modern traditions originated with these dates (for instance, Saint Brigit's Day, May Day and International Workers Day, Halloween, All Souls' Day). Because of my Irish heritage, I decided to use the names of that tradition: February 1, Imbolc, a celebration of new beginnings, truth, innocence, making plans; May 1, Beltane, the joys of fertility, growth, heroes and heroines; August 1, Lughnasadh, the harvest time, spiritual maturity; November 1, Samhain, the remembrance of ancestors, the thinning of the veil between the material and spiritual worlds.

What most impressed the women attending these ceremonies was that women of different ages, faith traditions, and ethnic backgrounds could come together to discuss and celebrate the important life and death features in their lives, in accordance with the themes of the cross quarters, and connect with the fifty thousand or so generations of humans who had also celebrated these times. Truly, it has been one more way of overcoming our "diaspora" under patriarchy. The works of Vicki Noble, Marija Gimbutas, Merlin Stone, Mary Daly, Caitlin Matthews, and others were essential encouragements to bring this first vision to reality.

In addition to this circle, I also initiated a circle of seven women priests from my own tradition. We meet regularly to meditate together, share a meal and laughter, and help one another become better priests. We contribute our stories of ministry, the solutions to problems we encounter, what questions arise, what we are teaching, and what we are learning. Another outgrowth of the cross quarter women's gatherings has been the development of "Menopause without Medicine" workshops and circles, where women who have successfully taken themselves through perimenopause with yoga, meditation, herbal remedies, and community have shared their experiences with others who are just starting the process.

Other participants in the cross quarters have gained confidence to begin their own spiritual circles. There has been a true spiraling out from what began in the spring of 2000 into meditation groups, shamanic circles, and other ways of bringing women together. The circles-within-circles image of the vision truly unfolded.

THE SECOND VISION

Within six months of my illness, I began to form the cooperative housing group by passing out flyers at social gatherings and by recruiting people through colleagues and friends. On Halloween of 2001, our Logan Square Housing Cooperative bought an eight-unit building where I now reside with eleven others. We are active in the community on a number of issues, including affordable housing. We advocate for the development of more cooperatives, we network with others on solving housing issues, and we organize education on the cooperative movement. The second vision materialized.

It took a year of regular biweekly meetings for the group to meld, for bylaws to be written, for consensus decision-making practice, for investigation into all the legal ramifications, for consultation with others who worked on co-op development, and for commitment to the financial and organizational structure to be made. This was no easy task. We all shared the common desire of creating stable home ownership in the midst of a great housing crisis in Chicago. We were all renters whose rents were increasing and who had to move frequently because of the development of expensive condos.

For a while it seemed there was a revolving door as people entered and left the process. Because of a family crisis, I also left for a while. But because of the strength of individuals and the wisdom of the group process, the Logan Square Cooperative was born.

Most of the people who live in the co-op have worked in social justice organizations and peace movements over the years. Some have long practice in the environmental movement, some have worked on homelessness for years, some work in higher education, some have put their energies into progressive electoral campaigns, and some have worked on accessibility for differently abled people. We bring a variety of strengths—and weaknesses, for that matter—to the table. It is an ongoing process in skill sharing and democratic decision making to allocate funds for different projects and to decide where we will put our energies together for the bonding and for the community we reside in now. It is as Gandhi described of his cooperative ventures: "an experiment in truth."

I also became more involved in researching women and peace efforts, studying global trends, and writing more. This prepared me for the ministry so needed when September 2001 and its aftermath hit. The interfaith efforts, my studies, community activities, and meditations also gave me the courage to dare to design college courses. (This was no small feat for a woman who started her political life as a welfare mother thirty years ago.) DePaul University recently hired me to teach two courses: Women's Voices in Peacemaking and Cooperatives: Building Communities of Peace and Justice.

THE BEGINNING OF THE THIRD VISION

My priesthood has blossomed in numerous ways since that encounter with myself in 1999. My studies of global trends, inspired by that third vision in the midst of my illness, uncovered facts that informed the actions I would take. I have published more articles, presided over more weddings and other rituals, advised more seminarians, and designed more consciousness workshops. I saw the demographic shift taking place in seminaries of nearly all traditions: women were entering in unprecedented numbers.

When asked to serve as an advisor to people in the seminary I had graduated from, I did not hesitate. This kind of mentorship serves both mentor and mentee by providing dialogue on spiritual matters. The weddings I performed became more creative, drawing on the rich ethnic traditions of the couples I was marrying as well as the universality of spiritual evolution. The articles I wrote more firmly tied spiritual concepts to today's realities.

By studying anthropology, politics, spirituality, philosophy, theories on education, and even physics, combined with meditation, I began to understand how and why women are taking the lead in peace and justice movements throughout the world. The revelations inherent in that third vision, so nebulous at the time, become clearer with each passing day.

Millions of people on this planet are awakening to their own true reality. I am not special in this regard. Had I not been so stubborn in putting off a lengthy retreat for myself, had I been more disciplined about longer meditations, had I had more confidence in my ability to work on communities of peace, perhaps the universe could have just whispered instead of shouted in that winter of illness.

My eyes have been opened to the great transformation taking place on our planet. After six thousand years of "power over" philosophy, the "power with" or "power to" philosophy is coming to the forefront once again. It has inspired the cooperative ventures of my life in housing, education, interfaith peace efforts, and consciousness raising. I am simply one person riding this surge, and contributing to this wave, of new awareness. What we are witnessing worldwide is a great turning away from violence as a solution to problems as women gain more collective spiritual, political, and social power (my grandmother was not allowed to vote until she was in her thirties because she was a woman). The twentieth century was the turning point. It was the bloodiest century in human history but it provoked pivotal factors that are now maturing. Starting about midway into that century (when I was born), the movement of nonviolence began to have significant impact.

Tens of millions of people were saved from slaughter as nonviolence traveled from independence for India to civil rights in America, to ending apartheid in South Africa, to the solidarity movement in Poland, to the overthrow of the Marcos regime in the Philippines, to Northern Ireland, to the downfall of totalitarian governments in South America, to the ending of war games in Vieques.

Women have participated as the majority of those working for nonviolent solutions, and many are unrecognized leaders in this global movement. It is no surprise, since women and children are now (unlike the victims of past centuries) the vast majority killed and injured in wars and now constitute the vast majority of refugees on this planet. I see more clearly now the dialectical relationship between the individual, community, and global nonviolence (*ahimsa* in my tradition), the role of women in this historic change, and the part I need to play. I know that the twenty-first century is shaping up to be the greatest showdown between the forces for peace and justice and those of war and oppression. I know that peace is the natural state of humanity and is becoming more and more a valued necessity for human organizing efforts, given the desperation of patriarchy and the reality of superpower imperialism. I know that it is a lie that war has always been with us. For tens of thousands of years people lived without this vehicle of patriarchal accumulation. I now spend my time giving hope to myself and others by reminding people that war is a social construct and peace is our natural state.

The great lesson that came through for me was this: when I allow spirit to flow through me, unimpeded by petty desires and ego-ridden lack of self-esteem; when I take my blinders off by giving myself moments of timelessness and by turning away from momentary sensual distractions; when I allow myself to be of greater service in community, I see further with more clarity and am able to write larger on the planet for the betterment of all beings. I believe that this is a universal lesson as well as my own individual experience.

In a sense, my experience in 1999 was just another tap on the shoulder from the Goddess of Creating, Maintaining, and Dissolving, from the Buddha, from God, from Allah, from Yahweh, from Jesus, from the universal goodness. With the speeding up of our lives, with the acceleration of energies in the universe, with the need for increased self-conscious awareness, we are being asked to step forward as instruments of peace, to integrate our lives more fully in the values we espouse, and to work more efficiently and joyfully for peace and justice.

The present-day global nonviolence movement against war and corporate globalization needs every spiritual leader from every tradition so that the web does not break but only grows in strength and luminosity. Along with millions of others, I believe this is the time to study and work in the field of nonviolence. Our internationalism and interfaith movements feed nonviolence.

Do not wait for your bout with pneumonia or some other harsh wake-up call! Now is the time to become active for peace in the world. Throw off any hesitations, complacencies, or despairs. Move that ego out of the way. Every one of us can be a vehicle for goodness, light, and love. We are blessed with spiritual energies working through us and among us in mysterious and wondrous ways. Let us join our individual spiritual transformations together to create the peace of the twenty-first century. Meditate, and take more community action for the coming historic victory of peace on this planet.

Ethical Speech as a Spiritual Practice

Mirka Knaster

I T'S SO EASY TO COMPARTMENTALIZE spiritual practice. We pray at a synagogue, church, temple, or mosque. We celebrate religious holidays. We make a ritual offering. But how much do we take into account our daily interactions as a prime arena for expressing our tradition's core beliefs?

When I was first involved in Buddhism in the late 1970s, it did not occur to me that speech had anything to do with spiritual practice. Like most Westerners of my generation who adopted this Asian-born philosophy, I focused on sitting erect and still in a cross-legged position with eyes closed. The only thing that was likely to come out of my mouth was the breath, not words. The talking I engaged in was internal—an endless stream of imagined conversations, fantasies, memories, judgments, plans, rehearsals, and emotions. On the outside there was silence, but on the inside there was a chatterbox. Every so often there would be a momentary break in this flow of inner speech.

Yet, as meditation deepened, something soon became clear. In the quiet of concentration, certain past acts of speech or behavior spontaneously arose on the mind's inner screen, and I felt the compunction and disquiet of those recollections. It was not that I remembered murdering someone, robbing a bank, or drinking myself into a stupor. Rather, I recalled the myriad ways I'd deluded myself into justifying such disrespectful acts as hurling an unkind or angry word in reaction to feeling rejected, responding in a snide or sarcastic tone, or speaking about someone else in unflattering terms. Increasingly, it was the little things that came up for examination. I sensed that there was no way to commit unwholesome speech or deeds without paying an inner price. I experienced the remorse viscerally. While these acts weren't condemned socially, they were keeping me from wholehearted participation in the Buddha's teaching (the Dharma).

It wasn't so much a case of rigidly following prescribed precepts: "Don't do this! Don't do that!" Instead, it was about feeling the impact of the doing: smarting from the conflict between my words and my spiritual aspirations. Knowing that I'd hurt someone through my unconscious, un-thought-out remarks. Realizing that in hurting another I was hurting myself as well.

My spiritual practice soon took on a much larger context than my sitting cushion. I had felt safe in meditation, especially on intensive silent retreats, because I knew I wouldn't blurt out something foolish or damaging, something I'd be sorry for. Now I had to learn how to feel safe when talking, too. Gradually I came to appreciate that the Buddhist precept regarding wise or "right" speech was not a commandment but a guideline for living nonviolently and respectfully. But of the five major Buddhist precepts, restraint from unwise speech has proved the most challenging of all. (The five precepts are these: I undertake the training [precept] to refrain from destroying life. I undertake the training to refrain from taking what is not given. I undertake the training to refrain from sexual misconduct. I undertake the training to refrain from harsh, cruel, or impolite speech; gossip; or frivolous talk. I undertake the training to refrain from that which intoxicates the mind.)

One day, I was smacked broadside by not fully comprehending what that precept means. A dear friend called, upset about her partner's behavior vis-à-vis a woman friend of his. As a longtime "sister," I listened caringly. Although he did not hear what she and I said in our phone conversation, by "chance" he read my e-mail that followed it. I meant no harm. I thought I was being supportive of my friend. But it was careless communication on my part, and it cost me dearly—estrangement from my Dharma pal.

The painful repercussions of this experience awoke me to a simple fact: while I had been careful in watching the movement of breath in meditation, I had not been as attentive in watching the words coming out of my mouth (or my fingers in writing). I'd neglected an essential aspect of spiritual practice the world over: guarding the tongue.

Now I see that by using speech as a focal point, I naturally bring in the rest of the Buddha's teaching more easily. He taught a particular path to freedom that rests on three foundations: ethical conduct, meditation, and wisdom. Without attending to the ethics of bodily and verbal behavior, it's difficult to attain higher states of concentration because the mind is distracted by guilt. Without such concentration, it's hard to gain the insight that ultimately leads to liberation.

There are possible reasons why things unfolded in this way for me and for others who embraced the Dharma. Some Asian masters who came to teach in the West may have felt no need to explain what was expected in their home cultures, just as Jewish and Christian clergy might assume that everyone knows the Decalogue. Westerners returning from Asia and starting to teach at home didn't emphasize the moral pillar of the Buddha's teaching. We were a generation that had seriously questioned and rebelled against religious, political, and social authority. We wanted meditation, not more rules.

But as I have continued to learn about the Dharma, I understand better how wise speech is integral to the Noble Eightfold Path that the Buddha outlined for awakening. There isn't the remotest possibility of attaining enlightenment unless I speak from a heart of compassion and wisdom.

In Search of Myself

ROMUALD JAKUB WEKSLER-WASZKINEL

I WAS BORN DURING WORLD WAR II in the small town of Stare Święciany, near Vilnius (currently belonging to Lithuania). Before I started attending school, I had frequently seen my birth certificate stamped with a large Lithuanian seal. According to the certificate I was born on March 25, 1943. But when I went to school, the date was slightly different. Even though the year of my birth was the same, the month was altered: it was February 28. Naturally, I drew my parents' attention to that change, but the answer that I heard from my father was "You know, it was the war back then...."

I spent the years of elementary and high school in Pasłęk, a town that was incorporated in the Olsztyn district in the past. I remained an only child until I was nine, and then my sister was born. My family home was that of a poor metalworker, whose wife took care of a small farm: we had a cow, several hens, and sometimes pigs that were slaughtered on the occasion of Christmas or Easter.

Both my childhood and early youth were very similar to those of my peers, though at the same time I was slightly different from my friends. I was a child of poor health, and I also stuttered. Moreover, I was afraid of everything: geese, roosters, cows, and especially mice. When I was playing with other children and a plane appeared in the sky, I fell to the ground at its sight. Children laughed at my behavior, but my mother explained: "Don't be scared, they do not drop bombs any more." I didn't understand what it meant "to drop bombs," but the moment I heard the sound of the plane I clung to the ground instinctively.

I recall a certain event that made a profound impression on me. It must have been a beautiful July evening or late afternoon. (I wasn't attending school yet, so it might have been summertime in 1949.) I was on my way home when all of a sudden two men, standing on the opposite side of the street, yelled in my direction: "A Jew, Jewish *bajstruk*" (which means a foundling, a child without a father). I looked in their direction but they burst out laughing. I had no doubt this name was meant for me. But why did they shout "a Jew"? And why *bajstruk?* I had a mummy and a daddy who loved me very much!

Terrified and stuttering, I tried to explain to my mother what had actually happened. I sobbed bitterly, and I was scared. My mother kept asking me; "Who were those people that called you names?" When I asked why they called me a Jew and a foundling, she replied: "Good and wise people will not call you like that. And there is no need to listen to bad people."

From other difficult moments of my childhood I remember that I wasn't able to deal with the questions asked by my friends: "Who do you actually take after?" I resembled neither my father nor my mother. They had typically Polish, Slavic features—while I had dark curly hair, and everything in my face was somehow different from my parents' appearance.

Yet another memory is connected with searching for traces of resemblance to my parents, which has affected me to a large degree. As it turned out later, it also had an influence on my mother's behavior. It happened during the time when I was already in the fifth or sixth grade of my school. One day I was standing in front of a mirror and combing my hair. For a moment it seemed to me that I found in my face something that resembled my father's features and I burst out with the question: "Mum, look, I take after daddy, don't I?" But as my mother was an exceptionally truthful person, she did not confirm my "discovery."

So this sudden question was followed by heavy silence, which I broke with an outcry: "Because if I'm a Jew, you'll see what I'll do to myself!" After a while I looked more deeply into that mirror and saw tears in my mother's eyes. Suddenly I felt ashamed of myself. Even today I am ashamed at the words that I cried out that day.

In high school there weren't any problems. I was a good student. My parents were very proud of me. Adolescents do not pose questions like "Who do you take after?" Nobody called me a Jew in high school.

My parents were devout believers. We prayed together, and I regularly accompanied them in attending Sunday mass. I had been an altar boy since kindergarten, and since I can recall—I had always wanted to be a priest. I enjoyed being in church very much. More than other things, I remember the priest walking among people with a small basket and people throwing coins into it. When I also threw in some money, the priest would always pat my head gently. In the times of my early childhood it was my biggest religious experience.

However, in high school my enthusiasm subsided, and in the final grade it seemed to me that God was no longer needed. Anyway, my "heaven" was set on fire. Although I never revealed to my parents any signs of rebellion connected with my wavering faith I stopped thinking about becoming a priest.

Then suddenly, a few weeks before my final exams, while I was walking along the street with my catechist, I told him—or rather let it slip—that I would probably enter a seminary as soon as I graduated from high school. Just as I said that I got scared of my own words. That very evening I repeated the thing I'd said to the priest to my parents. And there came a total surprise! My father, who hardly ever missed a Sunday mass, who was extremely tired as he labored very hard, who never went to sleep without having knelt down to his prayers first, instead of revealing joy that his son would become a priest, started mocking me.

"You? A priest? And what are we going to do with all the girls that our house is so full of?" He was right: I always had lots of friends, I used to play an accordion, and while I was still in high school I never missed a party.

Nevertheless, I was very surprised by the attitude of my father who acknowledged my intention of becoming a priest with such a great dose of reserve, even unwillingness. On the other hand, it seemed that it was my father's approach that actually spurred me to go to the seminary despite any obstacles. My father was visibly discontented by my decision. My mother never said a word about it. I saw her stealthily wiping tears. When I asked her why she was crying, she replied that women sometimes behaved that way. Nevertheless, there was neither encouragement nor criticism on her part.

On September 15, 1960, I entered the seminary in Olsztyn. Suddenly, on October 20, my father died. This was a genuine shock for me, especially as he had just visited me in the seminary on the Sunday before the aforementioned date. What is more, he appeared to be reconciled with the whole situation. However, something that makes me unsettled to this very day took place. During his visit we both went to an empty seminary chapel. On the major wall there was a large picture devoted to the Virgin Mary (a painting that has been revered in Vilnius).

Just when he entered the chapel with me, my father knelt down and started to cry. I felt confused. When we left the chapel, I asked him why he was crying: Was he feeling unwell? Was he troubled by anything? He replied that he felt fine and was not worried. He told me that his tears were his own affair and that I shouldn't take them personally. This happened on Sunday, and on the following Thursday around 7 p.m. I received a phone call informing me that my father had died of a heart attack.

My first reaction was the urge to escape from the seminary. It seemed to me that I was guilty of my father's death. He didn't want me to become a priest. I had acted against his will. His behavior in the chapel was a message that was totally inexplicable for me. After my father's funeral, when I told my mother that perhaps I should not return to the seminary, she reacted very strongly. She said, "You should not blame yourself for your father's death. If you find your studies too hard, then you will come back, but you must not resign from school because of what happened."

After I arrived at the seminary I revealed my doubts to the rector. He said that I was in a heavy shock and in such a condition I shouldn't decide about leaving. If I still wanted to quit after a month I would be allowed to do it.

However, after this time passed, I decided that the whole situation was actually the reason for which I should not leave. And it wasn't my private affair any more. It had already "cost" the death of my father, so I had to prove to him that my decision had been made in earnest. If my father was afraid that I would be a bad priest it was up to me to prove that I could be a good one. And thus I decided to stay.

The years in the seminary passed very fast. There weren't any major problems concerning my studies, my colleagues or myself. Everything indicated that I would become a priest.

During the fifth year of theological studies there is usually an announcement in a home parish informing that such and such a candidate is about to be ordained. On that occasion, anybody who is familiar with any facts preventing the candidate from being ordained is obliged to inform the rector about it. After this information had been announced in every parish, the rector summoned all of us. While I went there absolutely calm, I left his room utterly shaken. Right at the very beginning of our conversation the rector told me that there were serious suspicions that I had not been baptized. Suddenly I felt dizzy. Who could not have been baptized if not a Jew? Maybe I was a Jew after all? I asked the rector how he had obtained such information. My godmother was still living. Also, I knew precisely who my godfather was. Besides, at home I frequently heard about my baptism, which had taken place on Easter, in 1943. I asked the rector what precise data he had about me. He said he didn't have anything, and he refused to comment further on the subject. Even though those were only suspicions, he wanted me to agree to receive a so-called conditional baptism. I dismissed this suggestion. I said that agreeing to conditional baptism would offend my parents, who were decent people and would never lie to me. Besides, I had received my First Communion and received the sacrament of confirmation—how would that have been possible without baptism? In the end, I asked the rector to agree to meet my godmother so she could cast away all doubts. This plan soon came to pass, and the whole affair subsided.

On June 19, 1966, I was ordained during the millennium ceremony in Warmia diocese, in Frombork Basilica. In August of that year I started to work in Kwidzyn, in the parish of the Holy Trinity. I worked there for a year. Once, a taxi driver who took me to a sick person asked me if I were aware of the fact that people called me a Jew. I asked him back if he were aware of the fact that Jesus was also a Jew. The dialogue stopped at this stage. Although I didn't feel pleased at all, I wasn't afraid of Jews any longer. I wasn't even afraid that I might be one of them. The Bible, which I had read and studied in the seminary, drew me closer to the Jewish world. The closeness of Jesus from Nazareth was the closeness of a Jew for me.

In 1968 I was sent to Lublin to work toward a degree in philosophy at the Catholic University there. After graduating I stayed at the university, and I have worked there up to the present moment. In 1975 both my mother and sister came to Lublin to live with me. The problem of Jewishness still accompanied me, though very discreetly. Once, one of my colleagues told me that he heard I was an orphan saved from the transport of Jews taken to Majdanek. I kept asking about the source of this information, but he refused to say anything else.

During this particular time I read a lot of so-called camp literature and Jewish memoirs from World War II. The thought that I might possibly be a Jewish child torn from death gradually matured inside me. I tried to speak with my mother about it, but she would never keep up the discussion. Rather, she invariably changed the subject, which was a sign that there must have been something to it. So I tried to talk about the years of the war, about the place of my birth. I raised numerous detailed questions. But the moment I asked about Jews, the conversation was abruptly over. I noticed a couple of times that she was wiping away tears. One day I abruptly stopped reading and asked her directly, "Mom, why are you crying? Am I a Jew?" Instead of an answer I heard a question, which she cried out loudly: "Don't I love you enough?" At that moment I also started to cry. I was not able to read any longer. Although she had not really given me an answer, this said enough. I learned nearly everything in 1978. My mother was briefly hospitalized because of what was suspected to be cancer. She must have felt that she would die soon. She lived eleven years longer though; she died on April 15 in 1989.

Still, our crucial conversation took place on Thursday, February 23, 1978. At dinner we talked about Stare Święciany during the war period. I mentioned some familiar streets and names, and then once again I asked about Jews—that is, if she had known any of them during the war. Then my mother broke down in tears. I took her hands and kissed them assuring her that she should tell me the whole truth. These were the most beautiful moments of her life, and they also hid the truth about my life. I explained that I was mature enough to endure the truth, and that I would manage to cope with it. Then, for the first time I heard, "You had wonderful parents. They loved you very much. They were Jews who were murdered. I only saved you from a similar death."

We were both crying, and the world changed around me. While remaining myself I was becoming somebody else. I asked my mother about my real name, but she didn't know it. She hadn't wanted to remember the name, as it would have been too dangerous. Somebody might have denounced us to the Germans, which could have resulted in persecution. And thus, not knowing my surname, she could always say: "He is my child and I love him." This was how my mother explained this. But why didn't she want me to find out the truth? Why was she hiding it from me? Then she reminded me of that day in front of the mirror, and my cry that if I were a Jew I would do something to myself. She said, "I love you no matter what, and I have never wanted you to hurt yourself because of that." That evening I heard something that was the most significant thing for me: the explanation of my father's death and my priesthood.

My Polish mother had wanted to adopt a child during the war years. She even considered taking a Jewish orphan but she was afraid to do that. My Polish parents didn't have their own flat; they only rented a room from a family. Keeping a Jewish child in such conditions was very difficult and, most of all, dangerous. Being discovered hiding a Jew could result in capital punishment.

I didn't ask about the circumstances in which my Polish mother had come across my Jewish family. My Jewish mother had used arguments that appealed to the Christian values of my Polish mother. As the latter declared herself to be a devout believer, my Jewish mother told her: "You emphasize the fact that you are a Christian, and that you believe in Jesus. He was a Jew. So try to save this Jewish baby for the Jew in whom you believe. And one day he will grow up to be a priest, and he will teach other people."

I heard my heart pounding in my chest. I had been a priest for twelve years already, and at that time I was thirty-five. At that moment I felt that I was born once again and that I was returning to myself. I understood the tears of my Polish father in the seminary chapel. It must have been difficult for him to believe that the prophecy of a terrified Jewish woman who wanted to save her child from death would be fulfilled in this way, in this child's life. Definitely, these words remain very precious for me also: they are the words of the Jewish mother in the life of her son, a Catholic priest. It was the beginning of my inward journey.

My Polish mother was familiar with the fact that my Jewish father was a tailor—actually a very good one, that being the reason for the Germans keeping him alive until 1943 while he worked for them. Moreover, my Polish mother remembered that I also had a brother named Samuel.

How could I discover other details? Had my Jewish family survived? Perhaps my brother was still living? Most of all, what was my real name? These were the questions that unsettled me. I was afraid to speak about my problem with anyone. However, in certain peculiar circumstances, I confided all this to a nun named Sister Klara Jaroszyńska, who had saved many Jews during the war and who had numerous contacts in Israel. This was how my correspondence with Israel started, although I didn't receive much response at that time. There were too many cases that were similar to mine. In the meantime my Polish mother died in my arms in 1989.

In 1992, Sister Klara went to Israel. Somebody suggested that perhaps a meeting of Jews from Stare Święciany who had survived the war could be arranged. This was a very good idea indeed. Soon it turned out that I was the son of Jacob and Batia Weksler and that I had a brother, Samuel. None of them survived the war, although my father's brother, Zwi Weksler, and sister, Rachel Weksler Sargowicz, lived in Israel in Nethanya in 1992. Rachel still lives there.

I went to Israel the same year. I was received with great affection and tears. My uncle, a deeply devout Jew, could not cope with the fact that I was a Catholic priest, but finally he accepted it.

I wanted my parents to be rewarded with the Medal for the Righteous in the World and immediately started the procedure. It wasn't easy: although my parents had saved a child from a Jewish family, did they save a Jew? Despite all the difficulties, this time it was my Jewish father's brother who helped me a great deal. He said: "He is a Catholic priest, but he loves Jews, and he has a great affection for his mother and father, as he has for his Jewish family." The fact that I was circumcised had crucial significance in this case.

In Yad Vashem, in 1995 I personally unveiled the memorial plate devoted to my Polish parents. My sister received the medal that her parents were awarded with.

My ID has my Jewish father's and mother's names: Jacob and Batia.

In Poland, there is a clear distinction between nationality and citizenship. In the blank space devoted to the latter, I've filled in the word: "POLISH." I wasn't sure what I should write in the blank with "nationality," so I asked a clerk what he would advise me to do, just to put him to the test. He replied: "You are a Catholic priest so you must be Polish." Then I asked, "And who were my parents?" He responded, "Jews." So I wrote, "Nationality: JEWISH."

This is how while living in Poland and being a Catholic priest I am of Jewish nationality. Reconciliation of those facts would be impossible for me to achieve in Israel. Thus, my Polish parents saved something of the Jew within me.

I Do

RAJAL REGAN

T ICK ... TOCK ... TICK ... TOCK. *My frantic, relentless mind races on, battling my sleep-deprived body. I stare blankly at the bedside clock as it finally reaches 5:15 a.m. Go time. For the better part of five hours my overactive mind has succumbed to the powers of wedding jitters as my body has tried desperately to replenish itself through sleep. It is a well-known fact that all brides obsess over their wedding day, and I especially have every right to—we're talking about a fourteen-hour affair, designed to please two families and three faiths. I anxiously hop out of bed (it is not as though I have been sleeping anyway) and head to the shower. The first wedding tradition common across faiths: the bride must always look magnificent.*

I first mentioned Matthew to my parents on a random visit home one fall. Just as I had expected, my parents' immediate reaction was "Absolutely not." Their dream and expectation was that I would marry a nice Indian boy, raised in the same Hindu traditions as myself. I had no problem with their plan, but love works in mysterious ways. The young man about whom I now tried to tell them, about whom I cared a great deal, was not at all what they had in mind.

One of their first objections came in the form of the question, "What about religion?" Matthew was raised in a Jewish-Catholic home, and therefore had a completely different religious foundation from mine. My parents tried to explain how difficult marriage would be for a couple with different faith traditions. They had such strong feelings about their own faith, that the idea of compromising between faiths was a great unknown to them, and, as with most unknowns in human nature, it was something to be feared. Despite their concerns, even they were unable to resist the calming effects of interfaith respect. They were quick to give Matthew some benefit of the doubt, simply based on his Jewish upbringing.

The makeup artist applies the finishing touches to my face and hair. What seem like hundreds of aunties ensure that my sari and jewelry are just right. The other bathrooms in the house are filled; my family crowds around the mirrors to make sure everyone looks his or her best on this special occasion. My grandmother chants a final prayer to ensure a most auspicious day. As I carry a traditional painted coconut, my uncle takes pictures of me leaving my parents' home for the last time as their little girl.

When I first brought my husband-to-be home to meet my parents, I wanted so badly for things to go smoothly, despite the worrisome, pessimistic voice inside my head. Hours seemed to pass as my dad took Matthew to lunch so that he could get to know him better. Over the course of their seven-hour lunch (a father cannot be too careful when interrogating potential suitors), Matthew explained to my father that he wanted to marry me, and asked for his blessing. My father voiced his many concerns. How will you raise your children? Will they learn to respect God? Will they be socially accepted? Will they be confused about their religious identity? Drawing on his own interfaith upbringing, Matthew began the difficult process of convincing my father that not only could an interfaith marriage work, but it had some unique benefits as well. His answers must have had a good effect on my father, for by the time our visit home was finished, my parents were happily ready to welcome Matthew into their family.

Nine a.m. Indian music echoes throughout the marble and glass entryway of the hotel as my cousins and Matthew's Indian friends try to fire up the groom's crowd for the *Baraat*. This is the entrance of the groom accompanied by singing, dancing, music, and fireworks. Normally the groom would arrive on a horse, but unfortunately horses aren't so easily accessible in downtown Houston in January. As the *Baraat* comes to a close Matthew is escorted to the wedding hall by my mother and aunt.

My cousins carry me into the ceremony and bring me to the *mandap,* where Matthew and both our parents await my arrival. The wedding ceremony takes place on the *mandap,* a special stage decorated with flowers and silk. When I enter the wedding hall I am taken aback by the beautiful decorations and all the flowers on the *mandap.* My wedding is just as I had imagined it would be.

As the Maharaj performs the ceremonies that make up a Hindu wedding he explains each step to Matthew, his family, and all of our guests, who together represent so many different backgrounds. For many of the people there, this is their first encounter with Hindu traditions, and they are enthralled. By the time the ceremony is complete and we are officially husband and wife, most of the guests have lost track of time, and at least another fifty people can be seen watching from windows that overlook the wedding hall.

A wedding is so many different things to so many people. It is an undeniably joyous occasion of monumental significance to just about every faith in the world. In other words, it is an event for which people have exact expectations, and those expectations are not quickly compromised.

There was no question for me, raised a Hindu, that I was going to be married by a Hindu priest in a traditional Hindu wedding. Coming from an interfaith family, Matthew's position was not as clearly defined. To accommodate our wishes and those of our families, we decided to have two weddings. The details of the second wedding were to be decided by Mathew.

Matthew was raised with a blend of Catholic and Jewish traditions. He attended both church and synagogue, respectively, on each religion's high holidays. His family celebrated both Christmas and Hanukkah. Matthew's faith evolved into a blend of the beliefs and traditions from both religions that he identified with most strongly. He was not comfortable choosing one over the other for fear of hurting one of his parents. So he decided to go the route of a civil ceremony, performed in the spirit of his two backgrounds. For the record, I was pulling for a Jewish wedding because I wanted to break a glass and do the chair dance!

The soothing, beautiful music of the harp fills the wedding hall, but despite its calming effects it is now my family's turn to be nervous. Although we have rehearsed the traditional Western ceremony twice the evening before, everyone is a bit nervous because this is their first time taking part in one. I have seen countless brides, in flowing white wedding dresses, walk down the aisle on television, in the movies, and even in person, but I never imagined that I would be the one. As we exchange our vows, cementing the lifelong commitment we had made just hours before, I know that I was meant to be with Matthew and that we will be able to understand and appreciate our differences in a way that will ultimately make us a stronger family.

Our wedding day represented the challenges we will always face to respect and accommodate our different faiths. As time passes I read more and more about Judaism. I feel that it has many common beliefs and philosophies with Hinduism. Matthew is also continually trying to learn as much as possible about Hinduism. We have been to services for all three of our faiths, indicating the importance we place on understanding each other's background.

When we have children, I want to be able to teach them about Hinduism, Judaism, and Catholicism. It is important that they appreciate who they are, and where they have come from. I know that if Matthew was able to have a normal childhood while being exposed to two religions, we can pull off three.

Applause thunders off the walls of the packed reception hall as Matthew and I enter while the MC announces the arrival of Mr. and Mrs. Matthew Regan. Both fathers, my brother, and several of our closest friends speak to the audience with much love and thoughtfulness. Their words make it clear to everyone that it is indeed possible to bridge differences with the basic virtues of the human spirit. As Matthew whispers the words of our song to me during our first dance, all of the anxiety that has built up over the last ten months of wedding planning is washed away.

Nearly two years have passed since we were married, and not a day has gone by that we have not experienced the effects of bringing multiple faiths into one family. At the end of the day, though, we are just that: a family. Our different backgrounds have not prevented us from building a strong and stable relationship, one that will continue to flourish as each day our life is enriched by our faiths. When I spoke the words "I do," I made a commitment not only to our relationship but also to bringing our faiths together in such a way that would only make us better people.

Spiritual Search

RORY MCENTEE

M Y SPIRITUAL SEARCHING BEGAN in earnest after my decision to return to Chicago in the summer of 2000, rather than attend law school at the University of Southern California the following fall. I was returning to Chicago for what I foresaw as spiritual training, though at the time I really didn't understand what that meant. Previously, in December 1999, I had attended the Parliament of the World's Religions in Cape Town, South Africa. There a friendship developed between Brother Wayne Teasdale and myself. I was returning to Chicago on his advice, and hoping to be able to spend as much time with him as possible. I consider myself quite blessed to have had the time with him that I did in Chicago, because the demand for his time throughout the world has grown tremendously since then.

In Chicago, Brother Wayne encouraged me to engage in a daily meditation practice. With fairly little instruction, I began meditating daily, and also at this time I began reading extensively within all the religious traditions. This led quite quickly to an initial awakening, including several of mystical experiences, culminating in a genuine insight into emptiness in early July of that summer.

This satori experience, perhaps best described as a grace, was preceded by a reflection on a mosquito. Earlier in the summer I had inquired of God what possible use a mosquito might have. The mosquito was flying around, stinging me and causing pain, and was totally un-aware of its actions, which struck me as quite humorous at the time. Silly little mosquito, I thought, so innocent, just flying around stinging people! Then, in the midst of a chuckle, I saw that this is the condition of us all. We are all wandering around this earth, unaware of our actions, hurting one another, and innocent. Then, in an instantaneous trans-mission (hence the use of the term "grace"), ignorance was removed, and I saw that all I had done in my life had come out of love, for love was all that existed. There was nothing other than this love. Everything, at its center, was simply the outpouring of love. There was nothing *doing* this outpouring, there was *only* this outpouring. At the center of everything was an empty hole, and out of this came the outpouring. I call this dynamic emptiness.

From this perspective it was easy to see how nothing had ever changed and that everything was the same as it had always been and al-ways would be. There was an eternal dimension to the insight. The dy-namic emptiness constituted what we are made of, even down to the physical level.

Interestingly, the outpouring associated with this dynamic empti-ness was revealed to me as love, but I remember thinking that it didn't necessarily have to be revealed as love. While the dynamic emptiness was eternal, constituting the hole and the outpouring, what the out-pouring reveals would seem to have infinite potential. This leads me to suggest that the revelation of emptiness could differ in some respects between individuals, groups, and species. In the case of the human race, the revelation of emptiness as love seems to be itself universal. It may represent a unique revelation of the Divine within the cosmos. Our human lives could be seen as an education in divine love, with which our experiences of human weakness, intimacy, and suffering are so tied.

This experience opened up for me, in a very concrete and percep-tible way, a whole new dimension of existence. One of its effects was to set my feet solidly on the path: instead of an aimless searching for something I did not quite understand, the journey became justified and concretized, and was given a greater sense of direction, confirmation, and urgency. In addition, it stamped out all hope that I would ever find true solace, peace, or happiness in the things of this world, breaking me free of any conceptual wanderings of the mind that might lead one to believe that the world could serve this purpose. My mystical experiences begged new questions from me and established a certain sense of responsibility, often viewed as a burden. What did they mean as far as my life journey was concerned? What did they mean as far as *others* were concerned? What, exactly, was God up to?

Here is a journal entry written a couple of weeks before the experience mentioned above as I struggled with these questions:

> I have recently had an explosion of mystical experiences. What do they mean? Well, that is beyond my knowledge (if I have any knowledge at all). Maybe I am being expanded to be able to accept more of the Divine, maybe not. I'm not sure if I should seek direction or just go with it. While all these have been extremely powerful experiences, I still return to our normal world, our normal waking consciousness. Are things different? Yes and no. I still wake up and have a hard time getting out of bed, I still get hungry, I still get mad at times, I still sometimes waste my time when I could be improving myself. The only yes I could slightly see is that every now and then I seem to think about things a little differently. When I get annoyed with someone I realize that I am annoyed with them and that this is a problem, my problem, to be worked on, rather than just being annoyed and turning that into a dislike for the person. I realize more when my mind wanders into useless thoughts, I realize a little more when I say things that are completely my ego and are even hurtful, I realize a little more often when my actions, words, and thoughts are unskillful, or not skillful enough. I guess it would be safe to say that I seem to be a little more aware.

Reflecting back on these experiences, I still say that the essential element in all of them seems to be an increase in awareness, which might be compared to viewing the world from a greater depth.

Since the time of that experience brought by the "silly little mosquito," I have sought direction, through both living teachers and the words of enlightened beings transmitted through books and videos. I cannot imagine my journey without the guidance I have received. Some of the beings whose words I have found helpful include Father Thomas Keating, His Holiness the Dalai Lama, Osho (Bagwhan Shree Rajneesh), Chogyam Trungpa, Krishnamurti, Brother Wayne Teasdale, Bernadette Roberts, Andrew Harvey, Ramana Maharshi, St. John of the Cross, Teresa of Avila, and Jim Marion. As a result of the tremendous amount of inauthentic spirituality that is being circulated today, I urge people to be very careful, intelligent, and discerning about any teacher from whom they seek direction. I mention the above names as sources of what I believe to be genuine spirituality.

As for my living teachers, there have been two root teachers: Brother Wayne Teasdale and Joshi Baba. Brother Wayne is a Catholic monk who has also been initiated as a *sannyāsi*, a wandering ascetic in the Hindu tradition. He has been a spiritual director for me as well as a close, close friend. His path might best be characterized as one of *presence, discernment,* and *surrender,* all contained within Jesus's words to the Father, "Your will, not mine, be done." We will explore this essential aspect of Christian spirituality in its relation to the other religious traditions later.

Joshi Baba is also a *sannyāsi*. I met him during an extended stay in India, in the most ordinary of circumstances. He had no followers and no indications that he was a teacher of any sort. I have spent only about a month with him, yet the depth of our friendship cannot be exaggerated. Joshi Baba, to me, embodies what I would like to refer to, with utmost tenderness, as a master. As I see it, a master is simply one form that an enlightened being may take, and there seems to be a qualitative difference in those whom existence chooses to be a master.

It will be difficult for me to name or describe or communicate this distinction, but perhaps it is enough simply to note it. The role of a master seems to be one of a mysterious portal into consciousness itself. While other teachers gave me direction, insight, and encouragement, my experience with Joshi was different. He was a portal that was always present and waiting for me. Yet, at the same time, our relationship was very grounded in this world. A deep, palpable, human communion took place, hallmarked by friendship, simplicity, and joy.

This experience gave me insight into a different dimension of the spiritual journey, one I have found similar descriptions of only in the literature of the guru traditions. In light of the guru problems that are so rampant in our world today, I hope not to glorify the position of a guru. At the same time, I think we need to be careful not to discount this experience of the spiritual life, which has benefited so many throughout history.

Experiences in the different faiths of Christianity, Buddhism, and Hinduism also have been central to my spiritual journey. I grew up Catholic, and my remembrance of a child's love of God will always be associated with the hymns and masses of the Catholic Church. I think that I grew up with a profound sense of God and my relationship with God. However, I never saw the church as necessarily involving my relationship with God, it was more that my relationship with God involved the church. I felt strongly, even at an early age, that most of the people teaching within the church, including the priests and religious folk, did not have such an intimate relationship with God themselves. I always thought that this put them in quite a deficient position to be teaching about God.

Later, as I began to study Buddhism after college, I felt that I was getting into something I could really sink my teeth into. Here was a religion, I felt, that was actually telling me how I could improve my relationship with God, and doing so in a very rational, psychologically astute, and direct manner. What could Christianity possibly offer to Buddhism, I began to think; at least they hadn't forgotten that enlightenment exists.

However, this phase was not to last long, and through my experience with Brother Wayne, as well as exposure to Father Thomas Keating's writings, I began to see that there is a hidden wisdom within the Catholic Church. Sadly, I believe this wisdom has been lost in much of Christianity today, but we can be grateful for those who have kept it alive and growing.

I also traveled to India, going deeper into Hinduism and Buddhism. I began to see that they were not perfect religions either and that each religion seemed to have ways in which it surpassed the others. How interesting it will be to see how all of these gifts interact as the religions become more intimate with one another. It is quite an exciting time, and in that spirit I would like to offer some of my reflections on these gifts.

Buddhism has always seemed to me the most intelligent of the religions. It has made unsurpassed use of our rational, analytical abilities to directly cultivate compassion and insight. It has also been engaged for millennia in an intense, scientific investigation of the mind. Having used the analytical part of the mind extensively in college (I majored in math) I felt a certain affinity with Buddhism in this regard. I believe that many Western scientists have also felt a similar affinity, and Buddhism has served as a natural leader in bridging the gap between science and religion. The Buddha himself encouraged critical thinking among his disciples and expounded his teachings in a very methodical, well-thought-out, and direct manner. A testament to Buddhism's supreme intelligence and its subsequent control over negative emotions can be found in the fact that it has never fought a war in the name of religion.

Hinduism's greatest accomplishment, to me, is its worldview. Hinduism cannot be separated from the culture of India, and in India we find a tremendous openness to the spiritual journey. India has developed the understanding that the spiritual journey is the destination of all people. While this teaching is present in mystical traditions the world over, in India it has penetrated the very fabric of society. It permeates the general population and does not remain confined to only those who are religiously minded. Indian philosophy speaks of life as a series of stages, eventually culminating in a life dedicated to the search for Truth, or the Self. You do not have to travel far in India to see the effects of this, as there are literally millions of wandering *sannyāsi* all throughout the country. These people have left behind all possessions, and they count on the generosity of others to support them in their religious quest. They serve as daily reminders to the Indian people that life culminates not in the acquisition of possessions or fame but in an intense search for God, filled with an abandonment of all that is of this world, and the resulting simplicity of life.

One of Christianity's gifts lies in its intimate ties to *this* world, perhaps stemming in part from its roots in Judaism. Christianity's long tradition of social work, charity, and service to the poor speaks volumes for its heart. These acts show that despite its failings throughout the years, a deep connection to the Divine remains. My favorite gift of Christianity, however, is its unique orientation to the spiritual path. As mentioned before, it is ultimately concerned with doing, or following, God's will. This includes elements of *presence, discernment,* and *surrender.*

I would argue that this orientation allows Christianity a certain freedom of movement within its own philosophy, theology, and understanding of the path. Christianity is not a closed or complete system, but one that is ever open to the mystery of God's work in the world, onto which no boundaries can be placed. As a direct result of this, I feel that Christianity contains within itself a tremendous capacity for a synthetic and integrative understanding of the other religions. I have felt in particular that the Spirit is now calling the Catholic Church to use this unique gift, and to reinvent itself in light of the revelations that the other religious traditions have to offer. This gift might also be used to unify the religions in a more coherent way, and it may be unique to the Catholic Church itself.

Interspirituality: The Next Wave of Consciousness

Russill Paul

MY OWN INTERSPIRITUAL DEVELOPMENT

My own path toward interspirituality began in childhood. It started out somewhat ambiguously. I was born in a Catholic home in South India but grew up in an orthodox Hindu neighborhood. India, like most of Asia, is only two percent Christian. In my neighborhood, there was only one other Christian family. I even went to a Hindu school for the first years of my schooling. Again, I knew only one other Christian boy on campus. My childhood is rich in nostalgic memories of celebrating all the Hindu festivals with my friends, but I could not openly practice Hindu customs for fear of offending my parents. Deep down I wanted to be Hindu; I actually felt Hindu, but I did not know how to lay claim to this urge.

My wife, Asha, had a very similar childhood; she, like me, was born in a Catholic family. Fortunately, her family maintained many Hindu customs and traditions. Another plus was the openness her father bore toward Hinduism. He even worshiped when at a Hindu shrine or temple. Such openness is rare among converts in India, who are taught to believe, as my father was, that Hinduism is a false tradition.

At home, my Roman Catholic parents were among the converts who believed that Hinduism was a false tradition. Hindus, for them, were devil worshipers. They made fun of my Hindu habits, especially my choice of being vegan, sitting on the floor in traditional Hindu style for my meals, and relishing kosher Hindu food that was often purchased for me from a kosher Hindu restaurant. I was also devouring enormous quantities of children's literature on Hinduism, which I borrowed from several different libraries that my father belonged to. Finally they panicked. When I was in my early teens, they whisked me off to a Catholic school, even selling their home in that Hindu neighborhood and purchasing another near the school so that I could get a Christian education.

I wasn't a bit interested in religion in my teens. My friends and I called ourselves "outstanding Catholics." We stood outside in the church yard rolling our joints; the service was not intoxicating enough. I am grateful, though, to the Salesian Brothers who imparted many wonderful qualities to me. It just didn't show at that time. Throughout my teens I did everything a wild teen would do, and I'm glad that I did because it paved the way for me to embrace the spiritual path in a truly radical way.

In my late teens I was deeply moved by the poverty around me in India, and I turned to the Gospels for insight. For the first time I actually heard the message of Jesus and knew that I had to give up everything and go follow him. Although I aspired to become a professional musician, I knew in my heart that nothing would truly satisfy me until I discovered the divine mystery that pervaded all of life, poverty included. I needed to know the mystery that Jesus himself knew. One day, I wound up all my affairs, called a family forum, and formally renounced the world to become a monk at Bede Griffiths's Christian ashram in Tamilnadu, South India. The term is an anomaly. How do Hinduism and Christianity go together in the same monastery?

The fact that Bede wore the ochre robes of a Hindu monk and that we chanted in Sanskrit upset my mother. It was no use telling her that this was a Benedictine monastery in the Catholic Church. Conservative local church groups, called the laity movement, had already tarnished the name of the ashram in my city. When I visited home, my mother would caution me that standing on my head in yoga asana was "of the devil."

At the ashram I discovered that my passion for music could be channeled through a formal spiritual discipline using sound as a yoga practice. A whole new world opened up for me. Sanskrit chanting, South Indian classical music, yoga, meditation—all these things felt as natural as breathing air. I had found my path. I was both a Benedictine monk and a yogi in the jungle. What an amazing combination! I never gave up being Christian, which is why I retain my birth name to the present day. I don't ever want to deny the tradition of my birth because I believe that there was a reason for my being born in a Christian home, and I will always honor that choice of my soul. In my adulthood I have discovered interspirituality as the most natural and authentic form of living out the fullness of my spiritual life in the world. Through it, I feel that I have become a world soul.

THE YOGA OF SOUND: THE FORM OF MY INTERSPIRITUAL PRACTICE

Sound and music have been closely related to the development of consciousness from the earliest of times. Hinduism offers the world one of the most sophisticated forms of a sonic theology and cosmology, backed by a tremendous collection of sonically related spiritual practices. In my work, the Yoga of Sound, I have identified four distinct types of sonic mysticism that can be tied to traditional streams of Hindu mysticism. I use the term "Yoga of Sound" to teach these forms of sonic mysticism, which I have found extremely valuable for our present time in history and particularly valuable for the West. Consciousness finds its expression on the material plane through our voices and through our music. What is more, current discoveries in science and medicine are validating the knowledge of this age-old system of spiritual health, which comes to us through an uninterrupted legacy of thirty-five hundred years.

The Yoga of Sound offers valuable insights to the practitioner of any spiritual path. This means that the principles of this path may be applied to the chant and meditation practices of any tradition. Because of the dynamism of this type of yoga, my own interspiritual journey has moved me rhythmically through a swelling and a dissolving, a deepening and a ripening, an appreciating and a critiquing, a seeking and a finding. Practicing the Yoga of Sound in an interspiritual framework has opened me to the Sufi tradition and also the Sikh tradition, both of which have their own types of sonic mysticism, which was originally inspired by Hindu methods. For me, the interspiritual path is truly the most effective way of living the paradox that is life itself. There is no doubt in my mind that the Divine is an interspiritual being. If not, why do we have so many different traditions?

Listen to a film soundtrack or a popular music recording from almost any country in the world, and you will notice many common musical arrangements, visual concepts, and production designs. Yet, there is a distinctive ethnic character, or flavor, in these regional adaptations. Individuality is not lost in the fusion of cultures, and the globalization of spirituality does not necessarily mean that individual traditions will be distorted or watered down to a mishmash of adulterated methods. Obviously there is this danger, but evolution is pushing traditional spiritualities to evolve into distinct forms within interspirituality. Traditional methods will continue in their purity, but our perspective of these traditional methods will change as our judgments become appreciations and our fears translate into understanding. The more this happens, the more generations of bigotry and prejudice will be transformed into acceptance. "Of this I am certain," wrote Walter de la Mare, "that it will be impossible for me to free myself, to escape from this world, unless in peace and amity I can take every shred of it, every friend and every enemy, all that these eyes have seen, these senses have discovered. This I *know*."

DANGERS AND DELIGHTS OF THE INTERSPIRITUAL PATH

The greatest danger of the interspiritual path is a dilettante attitude that outwardly embraces traditions but does not truly value their depth. People sometimes tend to lay claim to a tradition without truly engaging in it. The same, of course, can happen in conventional religions. A practitioner may be Catholic or Jewish but not truly practice the essential teachings of that tradition.

The other danger is adopting a potpourri mixture of unrelated practices and teachings, or a jarring combination of methods that don't really blend well. Let us keep in mind that all traditions began this way. It took time for each tradition to develop its methods. We must therefore be patient with the interspiritual process and allow it to evolve and mature through our personal commitment to authenticity.

I believe that interspirituality is an essential step toward our species consciously becoming a global community. Globalization has already happened in world music and world economy; what we now perceive taking place in America, and also in other parts of the Western world, is a melding of spiritual styles. This fusion of spiritual paths is fortifying the roots of interspirituality.

Interspirituality is often mistaken for a "mix and match" approach to patching together a convenient and personal "spiritual menu" for the week. This is far from the truth. The true interspiritual path is the authentic engagement of belonging to more than one tradition at the same time. Just as global culture, music, and economics were generated by Western incentive, evidence of the interspiritual movement now taking place in the West is indicative of the interspiritual age that is now upon us. It is the next wave in human consciousness.

RECOGNIZING THE SELF IN THE OTHER THROUGH SACRED PARTNERSHIP

The fear of interspirituality, which is a fear of spiritual globalization, is reflective of the most basic fear we all have: Will any semblance of our own lives and impressions remain when we merge with the Divine at death? Which parts of us survive when we move beyond this world? Bede Griffiths wrote in *Return to the Center*: "Creation loses any meaning if there are no distinctions in the ultimate state. If everything and everyone is 'lost' in God, even God himself will be lost in the One." Through an emerging global awareness, the Divine is showing us that our identity is not lost but merges with all things. These distinctions within unity already exist underneath the appearances of all forms, but we rediscover it anew when we allow our own spirituality to develop relationships with other spiritualities. Bede Griffiths again: "Eternity will be present there in its total reality, not in general, but in particular; each of us totally present to himself or herself in our eternal ground of being, body and soul."

The ideal relationship between our spiritualities, particularly in evolutionary terms, is through sacred partnership. Marriage has been relevant until now as a survival mechanism; in similar fashion, monotheistic religions have ensured their own survival by preventing their followers from exploring other traditions. This is not to say that either marriage or monotheism is no longer relevant, but that the two are due to embark on an evolutionary path. As Gary Zukav has eloquently explained in *Seat of the Soul,* marriage has not traditionally been a relationship between equals. The man has protected the woman; the woman has been dependent upon him, served his needs, and raised his children. This has been the patriarchal view of marriage for many millennia, and monotheistic religions have protected the institution of monogamous marriage in the same way that they have protected their own spiritualities—by discouraging their followers from exploring other traditions so that it was difficult if not impossible to arrive at understanding and respect.

Spouses who don't allow their marriage partners to relate (in friendship of course, not in sexual intimacy) with other individuals— either of the same or the opposite sex, are controlling in their approach to relationship. With abuse and isolation, they lay exclusive, jealous claim to their partners. Unfortunately, the leaders of many of the world's religions have laid this same kind of jealous claim to their followers.

Sacred partnership is a coming together of equals who are consciously aware that they need each other for their individual growth and for the common evolution of their species. When we enter into sacred partnership with other traditions, we discover, as we do in sacred partnership with other individuals, that we find ourselves in the other. We see our own tradition in the context of other traditions and other traditions in the context of our own. This type of partnership proportionally results in our seeing our own light or darkness in the light or darkness of other traditions, and vice versa.

The problem we have faced for the past two thousand years with the development of many of the world's great religions is that the immensity of the light that broke through each of the revelations of their founding spiritual masters blinded many of the newly awakened followers of those traditions. Overwhelmed with the brilliance and luminosity of their own light, they failed to realize that it was the same Light that had broken through the other traditions as well. Centuries have been spent devising reasons for defending the belief that the One Light reflected in a particular tradition was the true light; all others were false, or lesser. To further establish their arguments, practitioners became habituated to comparing the light in their own tradition with the shadow or darkness of the other traditions. Such projections have prevented many of the world's religious leaders from acknowledging the darkness and shadow in their own traditions.

It is no longer possible to ignore the shadow side of our religious traditions. We are now acutely aware of the limitations in every tradition, which can be compared side by side with the limitations of other traditions. Psychology has taught us that our inability to accept the shadow in ourselves and in our human relationships narrows us to make comparisons between our own light—our positive qualities—and the negative qualities, or darkness, of others. We then enter into blame, judgment, and prejudice. We fear relationships because we fear losing our light to the other person's shadow. Yet, when we lay aside our prejudices and embrace the whole person, or tradition, we discover a fullness of being in which nothing is lost. Our own shadow and the shadow of the other person are transformed by the increased luminosity of our own light merging with the light of the other. Bede Griffiths elucidates: "Our differences are lost only to their finite, separate mode of being but found in their eternal truth."

All is well. All will be well, and all manner of things will be well.

Julian of Norwich

Witness

A. Frell-Levy

If I could I surely would stand on the rock where Moses stood.

Spiritual

W HEN I WAS LITTLE, my Polish Catholic nanny invited me to Easter Mass. She had taken me to mass before. I knew how to cross myself, how to retain poise on my knees. I had acclimated to the rituals, to the reliable cast of characters, and to the predictable cadences: "The Lord be with you / and also with you." I had reported to my mother that I liked the services, and my mother, who had long ago been Catholic herself, in some sense enjoyed indulging my involvement.

My parents' household was governed by extravagance and reason. Janina, my nanny, provided me with a culturally different second home. Janina cooked *sledzie;* my dad made steak. Janina had lacy curtains and listened to country music; my mom hung drapes and played opera. Similarly, I considered *Jezus Chrystus* to be an artifact of Janina's home, akin to the flowery dishes and the brown couches, something that the decor and landscape of my parents' household simply would not accommodate. At home, I did not think about Jesus; he simply had no territory.

If there was no Jesus in my parents' house, there were no permissible religious questions at Janina's. It was an unfortunate and altogether too common polemic: belief was the opposite of reason. I was four years old, and my hands were always in two places; I was the subject of two apparently incongruous languages. My confusion translated in a curious way: I asked Janina's daughter why, if she was a Christian, she didn't bear nails through her hands. Then, in response to Janina's invitation to Easter Mass, I inquired, "If I go to church on Easter, how long will I have to stay on the cross?"

Given the problematic division between belief and reason, my instinct to crucify Christians—myself included—was, I believe, intrinsically religious. I refused to forfeit my intellect to my faith, or vice versa; instead, I required a complete religious experience encompassing both intellect and faith. I accomplished this by situating myself neither as a participant (where my belief would eclipse my reason) nor as a non-participant (where my reason would trump my belief) but rather as a corporeal witness. My heart could deny; my mind could deny; in the wings, my parents and Janina could shout their chorus of conflicting requirements. But on Easter morning, my four-year-old hands and feet nailed to the cross, my body would know the truth.

According to family tradition, my name should have been Rose, or Reise, after my Jewish grandmother and hers before that. She was a narcissistic woman, my grandmother, always waiting her turn in conversations; she was extravagant or, more accurately, a shell of extravagance, proclaiming her importance once it no longer spoke for itself. She moved to Chicago when I was eight, and we became close; we were two of a kind in our loneliness.

I should be clear: we had very little in common. She was a terrible listener; I was sullen and terse. I spent lunches at her retirement home drinking tepid tea and elongating my syllables so as to make myself audible. She told me stories in which she was perpetually situated as the compromised heroine: "I could have been a famous opera singer! Everyone loved me!" Rose wore a nightgown covered in sequins to her ninetieth birthday party; at this point, her audacity was beginning to mix rather dangerously with senility. Her usual after-dinner concerts had started to regress; show tunes were replaced by her childhood's Jewish melodies. I listened, entranced.

As my grandmother died I sang spirituals into her opaque eyes:

"City Called Heaven," "Give Me Jesus," "Steal Away." I tacitly begged her forgiveness; Rose had professed a lifelong hatred of all things Christian. But the spirituals stood as the unequivocal language of my grief: "My lord calls me; he calls me like the thunder; a trumpet sounds within my soul; I ain't got long to stay here." I sang her blood still in what I knew to be the wrong language as well as the only language.

I was sixteen, and my religious life had reached new heights of ambivalence. I quoted Nietzsche—"That something is irrational is not an argument against its existence but rather a condition for it"—and simultaneously derided anyone claiming a voice outside of the confines of logic. Secretly, I prayed. Secretly, I feared Jesus. He had become, in the later years of my childhood, an instrument of my personal alienation. Janina had excluded me from taking communion because I had not ceremoniously received my First Communion at age seven. My response had been nearly violent: how could I, a child whose religious instinct had once inspired her to literally mount the cross, be denied the ritual of communion?

The issue, in fact, had not changed: I could not engage religion if I could not engage my body. I took to writing symbols and words that I deemed meaningful on my skin: *Teiresias* (a blind, androgynous mythical prophet) in Greek, *mutashakira* (grateful) in Arabic, the alchemical sign for distillation. The most solid appropriation was, for me, the bodily inscription, the variant stigmata.

In his book entitled *The Genealogies of Religion*, Talal Asad claims that "it is a modern idea that a practitioner cannot know how to live religiously without being able to articulate that knowledge." I was indeed wedded to articulation; I considered it a condition of legitimacy. As my childhood Christianity rose like a question, the answer was always articulated in the body, first in wound, then in writing. First, I was situated on the cross, the text rising from my hands and feet—*Eloi, Eloi, lama sabachthani?*—and then my body held the narrative, like math, like something not yet decoded.

Jews are supposed to be buried intact, whole, awaiting resurrection. Rose, who always walked the edge of religious devotion, requested cremation. She approached the notion of afterlife with complete indifference. When I sang to her, I stopped when she died, the cadences losing all meaning when I became alone in the room. My own certainty that an afterlife did not exist had preceded even my theism; the body, after all, was the sine qua non of my religious experience.

> Remember that my life is a breath, my eye will never again see good.... As the cloud fades and vanishes, so those who go down to Sheol do not come up; they return no more to their houses, nor do their places know them any more. Therefore I will not restrain my mouth; I will speak in the anguish of my spirit; I will complain in the bitterness of my soul.
>
> Job 7:7, 9–11

In the Hebrew Bible, Job claims his voice as a prerogative of his mortality; his impermanence, in effect, is his fuel. His body determines the scope of his religiosity, and its articulation is, above all, active. When I was four years old, I understood my body to be the locus of my religiosity. For a long time, this meant demarcating the skin, bearing witness in wound and in symbol. Then my Judaism came to me—not as an idea, but as an imperative: *The Jewish body inflects its faith through doing.* And so it was that my body turned from canvas to agent, that the language of my witness changed.

Living Christ, Living Guru

BILL HAYASHI

For Gurumayi Chidvilasananda: "Om Guru Om"

I WAS BORN ON DECEMBER 2, 1941, in Santa Rosa, California, to Tanio and Shizue Hayashi, second-generation Japanese Americans. On December 7, five days later, the Japanese bombed Pearl Harbor. Four months later, my family and I were "prisoners of war" within our own country. The American government had decided, "for the protection of the nation," to place all Japanese West Coast inhabitants, whether they were American citizens or not, into these war camps, totally violating the rights of citizenship, not to mention human justice and decency. I remember the barbed wire fencing and the constant undertone of fear and shame. I learned at an early age that it was not "cool" to be Japanese.

When we were released from the camp some three years later, my parents were afraid to return immediately to California, so we moved instead to Roy, Utah. It was there that I had my first "religious" experience. My parents kept a Buddhist shrine in our bedroom, used more to honor the ancestors than to invoke the sacred. One morning I noticed that the ivory statue of Buddha had moved during the night and was now facing a different direction than what I had seen before going to bed. When I asked my parents whether or not they had touched the statue, they denied doing so and immediately righted it. We were all disconcerted the next morning when once again the Buddha had changed position. After several days of this "miracle," my parents decided to stay up all night to see what was really happening. It seems that at 4:30 a.m., a train passed by our house, which stood close to the tracks, rattling the wooden stand on which the Buddha sat and gently moving it. Although this explanation satisfied my parents, what most stayed with me was the sense of awe, terror, and wonder that first accompanied my early morning epiphanies. I believe this was my first experience of the mystical and transcendent, my introduction to something greater than the human mind could ever hope to explain or reify.

My first encounter with Christianity came when I was six. By that time we had returned to California and my parents were caretakers of a peach orchard for a wealthy white man. One day two Christian Missionary Alliance ladies showed up at the orchard and informed my parents that if they did not send me to Sunday School, I would certainly end up damned and in hell. Though they were practicing Buddhists, in name anyway, Mom and Dad let themselves be bullied, quietly deferring to white authority, and I soon found myself in regular attendance at the Christian Missionary Bible school. I actually really enjoyed it. I liked identifying with a white God-man "who died for my sins." I had never experienced pure, unconditional love from my parents, and singing the words "Jesus loves me this I know, for the Bible tells me so" gave me my first experience of sweet and conditionless acceptance. When I first heard the Easter story of the stone being removed from the cave and the tomb being empty, I recalled the awe and wonder of the mysteriously moving Buddha statue and hoped that no rational explanation would once again intrude to challenge this wondrous mystery.

My understanding of Christ continued in this way: a combination of father-hunger and racial projection (ideal image merger) along with true seeking, until I attended a weeklong conference with Reverend Paul Nagano at the Mount Herman Conference Center in Santa Cruz, California. It was an evangelical camp, and I soon found myself going forward to testify to the presence of the Holy Ghost within my soul and being. I did, indeed, experience something mysterious and profound enter me. For some years after that, I would honor the Spirit and glorify the Lord through spontaneous prayer and witnessing my story. Spirit spoke and moved within me. It was no longer a fantasy projection; I developed an intimate relationship with the living Christ. Jesus became my closest friend and confidant. I would speak with him almost continuously, especially when I had difficulties or fears, often in silence. He never failed to calm and soothe me. I felt supported, fearless, unstoppable. It was then that one of the truly defining moments of my life occurred.

When I was fourteen, my mother developed a serious heart condition and needed to have heart surgery. I felt totally confident that she would be fine because I prayed to Jesus and asked him to take care of her. When she died on the operating table, I felt that my world had stopped. Not only had I lost the person I felt closest to in this world, but I also felt let down by my best friend and trusted confidant. I tried to rationalize this betrayal by saying that if I had just said "Thy will be done" rather than directly asking him to save my mother, all might have been well. But I remained unconvinced at the deepest level. Though I continued to attend church and to pray publicly, in the space of "the sacred Yes," trust was broken. All inner conversation with Christ stopped. In the innermost space of the heart, I shut down to vulnerability and to divine surrender.

This became clear when I went away to college and found easy distraction. I stopped attending church and praying altogether. When I ask myself now, where did my longing for Spirit go, I realize it was channeled into my passion for music and literature. I had been playing classical piano since I was eight, and I soon immersed myself completely in scales, arpeggios, and Bach. The music room became my sanctuary and Mozart and Chopin my evangelists. When I completely lost myself in the music, Spirit once again came alive for me. All time and space would fall away, and I would no longer play Bach but Bach would play me. For a brief time, I would feel whole, complete, and one with the Light.

Another defining moment occurred when I was a sophomore studying in France. One day, on the student bulletin board, alongside requests for rides to Paris or for spring break companions to Rome, I noticed an index card with the following words neatly printed on it:

This above all: to thine own self be true,
And it must follow as the night the day
Thou canst not then be false to any man.

Shakespeare

Once again, the world stopped for me. These verses went deep into my being. The longing for authentic selfhood was born. I quickly copied down the words. They soon reappeared above my desk to become my motto and inspiration. I began to study Shakespeare passionately. Indeed, I wrote my doctoral dissertation on Shakespeare's *Troilus and Cressida*. Shakespeare's poetry and his truth inspired and uplifted me. (In retrospect, I also realized that through studying Shakespeare, I hoped to prove beyond a shadow of a doubt my mastery of the English language, especially to those fools who would infuriatingly ask me, a native speaker, where I had learned to speak "such good English.") In addition, this interest in finding true selfhood explains my deep and continuing interest in psychology and my study and licensing in various modes of psychotherapy.

This passion for music, literature, and the self persisted through college and only began to waver in graduate school under the grind and utter cerebrality of English literary studies. I had stopped playing the piano and was beginning to feel that I was living only "from the neck up," when some casual acquaintances mentioned Transcendental Meditation. They spoke primarily of stress reduction and inner peace, but something about the words "meditation" and "transcendental" called to me. During my first experience with mantra and meditation, I experienced a stillness and wonder similar to the felt presence of the Buddha moving or Bach playing me. Though I didn't recognize it then, it was also the "silent intimacy" I had once felt with Christ.

After practicing meditation in this way for about fifteen hears, I learned about a great Siddha Guru, or fully realized meditation master from India, named Swami Muktananda. Muktananda's primary teaching was "Honor your Self, love your Self, respect your Self, kneel to your Self, because God dwells within you as you." Here was someone telling me that my self was not only authentic and true but divine and eternal as well. I learned that Swami Muktananda had the gift of bestowing *shaktipat diksha*, or kundalini awakening: initiation into the journey of enlightenment. I decided I wanted to have this experience, so I arranged to receive *shaktipat*. Thus occurred the greatest defining moment of this or any of my lifetimes.

I sat in a room with hundreds of other seekers meditating with Swami Muktananda, who was sitting in a chair in front of us. As we sat there the room began to vibrate with an incredible energy, like the pressure of an electrical storm about to break. When I opened my eyes, I realized that this energy or power was emanating from Muktananda himself. At a certain point, Baba—or "father," as Muktananda is affectionately known—got up from his chair and began tapping people with a peacock feather wand and touching them in different places, at the base of the spine or on the heart chakra or on the third eye. As he went around, people moaned or cried out, sometimes moving violently and involuntarily. As the sounds grew louder I began to feel frightened. At a certain point, I realized that Baba had entered my row and I could hear the swish, swish, swish of the peacock feathers getting closer and closer. In total panic, I placed my hands in front of my forehead and began to repeat an old Buddhist prayer, *"namuamidabutsu, namuamida-butus"*: "I take refuge in the Buddha, I take refuge in the Buddha." When Baba came and stood in front of me, he pulled my hands down forcibly and started pushing in on my third eye with great intensity. I felt as if I was going to fall over backward so I quickly reached out and grabbed hold of his foot. I didn't know at the time that the feet of the *Sadguru* are where the *shakti* or energy of the master, enters the earth and so are like powerhouses of kundalini and grace. As Baba pushed in on my third eye and I clutched desperately at his left foot, I felt as if an electrical circuit was completed, and suddenly, *ka-boom*, the top of my head felt like it was blown off, and powerful streams of white light began pouring into my body. At first it was so intense that I was truly frightened, but as the light began to move and penetrate into every cell of my being, I began to relax and to savor the fullness and sweetness of this liquid luminosity. At a certain point, I began to sway back and forth in utter contentment and bliss. I remember thinking, "Oh this is who I truly am, this light is my true self." At a certain point, I opened my eyes and realized that this same light was pouring out of everyone else, their essence and source as well. After about half an hour, the light went away and I began to cry, to really, really sob. I kept asking myself, "Why are you crying? Is it because the light went away?" "No." "Is it because Baba has left?" "No." After about an hour, a voice from the deepest part of my being said, "You're crying because for the first time in your life you know what it feels like to really, really love yourself." And I knew that that was true. Ever since my first introduction to unconditional love through Jesus, I had always wanted to love and accept myself totally and utterly, but always, especially after my estrangement from Christ, I identified with my weaknesses, my inadequacies, my doubts and fears. In this experience of *shaktipat diksha,* however, Baba Muktananda had shown me who I truly was—this pure, brilliant white light—and in the face of such beauty and such glory I could do nothing but love, honor, and even bow to my own self. Baba had also shown me that this great light was, indeed, the essence and source of everyone and everything, the One in the many. In honoring my self, then, I was honoring the self in each and every one of us.

I soon realized that *shaktipat* was a gift, an advance revelation of the end of the journey, but that to become established in it, there needed to be much work, dedication, and purification. Swami Muktananda left his body in 1980, and his great successor, Gurumayi Chidvilasananda, then became the living guru. It was she who brought out and worked on one of my deepest *samskaras,* or psychic wounds, one that originated with the relocation camp experience. Gurumayi began placing me with Japanese devotees, something that made me feel very uncomfortable. After all, I didn't want people to think I was Japanese. Sensing my discomfort, she continued to bring out my resistance.

Finally, she asked me to give a talk on the guru-disciple relationship to a group of visiting Japanese at Shree Muktananda Ashram in upstate New York. Right in the middle of the talk, Gurumayi entered the room and interrupted me. "Why are you being translated?" she asked. "Gurumayi, I'm third-generation Japanese American, and I don't know that much Japanese," I replied. "Well, you know, you can't change the way you look," she retorted, and abruptly she left the room. I could barely finish the talk. Her words went straight to my heart. My first thought was "You know, she's right; I can't change the way I look." And then the revelation came. There had been times when I really wanted to change the way I looked, when I wanted to be the "white American dream" so that I could date the prom queen, times when I wanted to change the shape of my eyes so that kids would stop teasing me by pulling their eyes back with their fingers and saying, "Ching, chong, china-man." In a flash I saw the depth of my own racial self-hatred, perpetuated by these early childhood memories. I began to weep as I began to ask my self, how can you love, honor and respect your self when you can't even accept the way you look? Later that evening, I told Gurumayi in the *darshan* line that I wanted to begin learning Japanese. She seemed greatly pleased as she gently brushed me with her peacock feathers.

Thus began a deep process of purification and self-acceptance. I began to study the Japanese language and to teach Japanese cinema. Through this latter, I began to realize that I was really much more Japanese than I had ever realized. I could understand the characters' motivations in ways my American students simply couldn't. I also began to appreciate some of the strong qualities of Japanese culture: the sensitivity to beauty and nature, the willingness to serve, the honoring of ties and responsibilities. In 1991, I went to Japan to do advance work for Gurumayi's visit there. I felt much more at home and at ease than I would ever have expected. I also met a very pure and traditional Japanese woman, Kiyomi Mori, with whom I fell in love. Ironically, it was the very qualities that I most associated with her Japaneseness that won my heart: her deep sincerity and purity; her unconditional loyalty and commitment; her quiet, deep self-possession. Within six months we were married. We now have a ten-year-old son, Kiyoshi Japendra, whom we are raising bilingually and who has none of my former ambivalence about his Japaneseness.

This is the great gift of a Siddha Guru. Not only do you receive *shaktipat* initiation, which shows you the pure self; you also have a constant companion and teacher to bring out and support you in purifying the *samskaras*, or tendencies that keep you limited and unfree. With my marriage to Kiyomi, I overcame another ancient wound. Because my parents died when I was quite young, my mother when I was fourteen and my father when I was seventeen, I had a deep fear of intimacy and commitment. Through recognizing my own inner wholeness and completeness through meditation and through my increasing belief in love through my surrender to the guru, I was able to entrust my heart to another person in complete commitment and total faith. Kiyomi and I invited Gurumayi to our wedding in Chicago in 1991. She was not able to attend but sent us instead this beautiful marriage blessing: "I will be with you in the form of your love for one another."

One final wound that Gurumayi has helped to heal is my longtime estrangement from Christ. During a two-day intensive meditation program entitled "Believe in Love," Gurumayi led us in a very deep and silent meditation. A vision occurred to me. I saw four figures of light standing before me, each one removing itself to reveal the next. The first was Gurumayi. The second was Swami Muktananda, her guru. The third was Bhagwan Nityananda, his guru. The fourth came as a total surprise. It was Jesus the Christ. I was shocked to see him and to feel the depth and intensity of my response. "Get away," I spat out, enraged. With infinite compassion and grace, Jesus looked at me and lovingly replied, "You know, I didn't betray you. You just didn't understand. It was time for your mother to leave this plane." When I heard these words, I somehow felt their truth. My heart began to slowly open again to the living Christ. Later, when the meditation was over, Gurumayi told us it had been an unusually deep meditation because many great beings had joined us, so attracted are they by the experience of love. This substantiated the truth of my vision and my reconciliation with the Christ.

When I returned to Chicago a few days later, I was told by a friend who had been cat sitting for me that my pet kitty, Darcy, had been vomiting and unable to eat and that I ought to take her to the vet right away. After examining her, the vet sadly informed me that Darcy had a large tumor in her stomach—a tumor so big, it was inoperable. She recommended putting Darcy to sleep. This was very difficult for me since Darcy had been my "transitional object," the sentient being who had inspired me to begin opening to love and connection again—perhaps the first being, besides the gurus, that I had let myself feel truly vulnerable toward since my mother's passing. Immediately I began to recall the circumstances around Mommy's death, and just as immediately I began to feel the presence of Christ within the room. I sensed that Christ was letting me know that he would be with me in Darcy's transition just as he had been during my mother's. As I held Darcy Kittycat and watched her spirit leave this plane, I felt myself being held in Jesus's embrace. I realized that indeed, during Mommy's death, Christ had been there for me had I but had the eyes to see, and now, thanks to the living guru, I was returning to those loving, trusting eyes and to the faith I had had as a boy.

For some time after this experience, I had some difficulty deciding to whom I ought to pray: Jesus, God, the guru? Now I am simply grateful that God, guru, and Christ are alive for and within me. Often times, I will simply utter the word "Beloved" and feel the sweet presence of the Divine enfolding me, not that different from the spirit of Bach playing through me or the mysterious movement of the Buddha calling me home, home to the Great Light, home to Source and to true self.

It is this recognition and honoring of true self that I have come to see as my life work or calling. Whether I am teaching a class, offering a therapy session, giving meditation instructions, or playing with my ten-year-old, my intention is to bring people to an understanding of who they truly are, of the great light shining inside them, of the boundless ocean of love and greatness within their own hearts. It is, indeed, my intention in writing this very essay. And it is because I am aware of the necessity of exploring our wounds, bringing light into our shadow places, and healing the leper and the cripple within that I share my story with such candor and faith. I have come to recognize and honor both the light and the brokenness, the glory and the fear, the saint and the frightened child within myself and all others, knowing full well that without the acknowledgment of the first, there can be no lasting hope for the second. The poet Galway Kinnell has said it very well:

> The bud
>
> stands for all things,
>
> even for those things that don't flower,
>
> for everything flowers, from within, of self-blessing;
>
> though sometimes it is necessary
>
> to re-teach a thing its loveliness.
>
> to put a hand on the brow
>
> of the flower,
>
> and retell it in words and in touch,
>
> it is lovely,
>
> until it flowers again from within, of self-blessing.

Just as Swami Muktananda placed his hand on my forehead and re-showed me the great light within my core, so too I hope that some resonance from my words can perhaps touch your spirits, soothe some inner wounds, so that you too can further your flowering from within through self-acceptance, self-blessing. This is my wish for you all.

My Path Back to Judaism Was Paved in Breakbeats: The Return of a Jewish B-Boy

Kevin Coval / Melek Yonin

A T SIXTEEN, I TOLD MY BEST FRIEND not to call me Jewish. We were in high school in a largely Jewish, northern suburban community of Chicago. I fancied myself more a Black Panther (i.e., Huey Newton and Bobby Seale) than a B'nai B'rith Youth Organization (BBYO) attendee. For three years I'd been reading and listening to things hidden from my secular and religious education: things about Africa and urban centers, about the miseducation of all peoples and as KRS-One announces in his 1989 classic cut "Why Is That?" I learned that Abraham, Moses, and the whole patriarchal lineage of Judaism was ... black.

On the day of my bar mitzvah, the night before I only memorized my haftarah from audiotapes, disconnected from its meaning, my family was told to leave the synagogue. Before I went on the bema the rabbi asked if I would continue with Jewish youth groups, confirmation, etc., and I said "Hell no!" He then informed us that since we were months (if not years) behind on payments to the shul, we should consider worship in another congregation.

My folks were divorced when I was seven. My mother worked two or three jobs to keep us in the "superb" suburban education system. My brother Eric and I were latchkey kids, circa 1984, mid-era Reaganomics, not receiving much trickle-down. After school we'd play stickball behind the Ace Hardware, with their sod bags as our bases. We'd imagine "ninja" after the kung fu flicks we'd watch weekends on Channel 50, chasing each other around the neighborhood, jumping from trees or behind parked cars, or we'd breakdance, mimicking moves from the movies we loved (*Beat Street, Breakin', Wild Style*). Movies that leaked into our suburban townhouse: hip-hop's first cultural exports, affecting a globe of kids outside of New York, from Nebraska to Hong Kong to South Africa and Holland, even the suburbs.

For many kids like us, hip-hop was our mother and father while they were off at work ensuring we had food and roof, and though sometimes they worked through nights, we had headphones and boom boxes to sing our lullabies. Mine was a mixed tape from a South Bronx crew called Boogie Down Productions, featuring the lyrics of KRS-One, the considered and self-proclaimed teacher of hip-hop. In well-crafted rhymes, which for those who don't remember meant storytelling, representing the block you lived on, when hip-hop was humble and poor and created by the dispossessed in postindustrial America, before bling and gangsta rap, before crack and corporate monopolized homogeny, I listened. Although white and Jewish and suburban, I listened and felt a connection not via experience so much as in sentiment. KRS-One, Chuck D, and other socially minded, community-conscious emcees spoke to a nation about being disenchanted, being othered, wanting to do something, to learn, to *fight the power*, with poetry and dance, visual and sonic art, with hip-hop.

Because of my socioeconomic situation, I felt I always had an other-side-of-the-tracks-type experience. I was privy to and enjoyed many of the privileges of upper/middle/white/class/culture. But at night, after school, leaving a friend's house in a gated community, with mom on psychotropics at home, snacks on the table, and endless resources for entertainment, I'd return to my area that, though very nice, was different. It was littered with old and seemingly discarded grandparents, newly divorced mothers, their children, Latinos new to the country, on busy streets, behind gas stations and convenience stores, in the back of shopping malls. We moved six times in ten years—sometimes unable to afford rent, sometimes fleeing debtors and angry landlords, sometimes my mom just needing to start again. If hip-hop articulates the visions of the "other," insists on the visibility of the unseen, then I felt in some way hip-hop was for me, too.

In Sunday School, I listened to biblical tales of justice, firsthand accounts of the Holocaust, stories of shtetls and pogroms and Holocaust. But Jewish justice and struggle I associated with history. My present was filled with Mercedes Benz cars, corporate lawyers, investment bankers, mall wives, American princes and princesses. To me Judaism was wealth and hypocrisy, a rhetorical exercise that allowed people to feel good about *tzedakah* (charity) but not require them to be *tzadiks* (righteous persons).

Hip-hop and frustration brought me to the library as a teenager. Many of my peers were playing drinking games in basements while their parents were away. Often I was the designated driver. I was not a nerd (I say this because often intellectual or artistic activity is associated only with the socially deficient), but I read poetry and social theory in the party's corners, at night, in classes. I read Malcolm's autobiography in my sophomore year, and later Lerone Bennet Jr.'s history. I read about black liberation, civil rights, radical thought. I was borrowing and bringing them into my English and history classes, waging intellectual battles with my teachers. First day of U.S. history class, junior year, I raised my hand and asked why only white men were on the wall. I told my English teacher her canon was too white and narrow. Where were James Baldwin and Sonia Sanchez?

Hip-hop was and continues to be a radicalizing force in the formation of my social and political consciousness, but it's had an equally important role in the formation of my spiritual and religious center. Hip-hop's literary predecessors, the black arts and beat movements, introduced me, in my first year of college, to Buddhism. The summer after my first year I interned in Washington, D.C., for a senator on

Capitol Hill. Quickly I became disinterested in the social-climbing interns and the affairs between corporations and politicians. I turned to reading. My uncle had given me two books before the summer began, *The Black Poets* anthology edited by Dudley Randall, where I read Amiri Baraka, and *On the Road* by Jack Keroauc, where I was introduced to Buddhism and spontaneous prose. I maintained sanity by "freestyling" near the Potomac River all that summer.

The following fall, I took a philosophy class on Buddhism. I read *The Jew in the Lotus,* and I now imagine many Jewish kids can tell a similar tale, but while reading this book I kept thinking, "Where and why were the weird, spiritual, mystical practices of Judaism hidden?" This book explored the similarities between Tibetan Buddhism and Jewish mysticism, but more than anything it awakened in me a dormant interest in the tradition of my birth.

In 1996, I spent Hanukkah in the Jewish ghetto in Venice, Italy. I walked into a community center, was greeted by a rabbi from Brooklyn, and was asked if I'd lay tefillin. He and his wife took me around to museums, recounted the history of ghettoization for European Jews, and showed me windows arched to signify hidden synagogues, which I thought, like Capoiera or wild-style graffiti letters, were expressions beneath the dominant culture's radar screen. On that Sabbath, I ate in a small, narrow room filled with food, candlelight, whisky, and vodka bottles, men with *pe'at* and *tsi-tsi,* women who could not shake my hand but sang and clapped and drank till roosters let out wails in the yard.

As I continued to hang in more Jewish circles I had associative flashes, like I was viewing Rorschach blots. Everything seemed to remind me of hip-hop. The Sabbath minyan in Italy was hip-hop's cipher, the creative, social space where headz (hip-hop practitioners) gather to build and create. In the summer of 1998, I traveled in a van with friends to the West Coast. We stopped at the Rainbow Gathering: 20,000 nuevo-hippies in a forest in Arizona, dancing, cooking, praying, playing music. Somewhere in this mayhem and beauty I found the Kosher kitchen and its Rabbi Pinny, who had accompanied yeshiva students from New Jersey. On the Sabbath, Jews and non-Jews danced, sang, ate, and gazed at the stars. The only other space where I'd seen a collective body move like that was at hip-hop shows when the DJ drops a cut that sends the crowd rising like rockets toward the ceiling, hands and fists beating invisible drums on the shoulders of bodies packed before them.

A year later I visited Rabbi Pinny, his family, and the Hasidic congregation in Montreal during Rosh Hashana and Yom Kippur. I fasted with them, bathed in the *mikva*, sacrificed chickens in 4 a.m. alleyways, drank, listened to stories, and ate kugels. On the night of Kol Nidre, everything clicked. I saw my people, Jews who looked like my relatives, pray that night like I'd never seen. They were davening, I learned later, but to me they were head nodding—swaying back and forth, submissive to the rhythm of prayer. And as it was when I went to my first basement party, now for the first time in my life in a Jewish setting, I felt (finally) at home.

Rabbi Pinny and others (most notably the work of Aryeh Kaplan) introduced me to Jewish Meditation, particularly *hizbodedueth*, or self-isolation, developed by Abraham Abulafia and others in thirteenth-century Spain, not long before the inquisition. Abulafia would wrap himself in tallit and tefillin and write spontaneously. He said,

> Begin to combine letters ... delight in how they move. When you feel very, very warm from combining the letters, and through the combinations you understand new things that you have not attained by human tradition nor discovered through your own mental reflection, then you are ready to receive the abundant flow, and the abundance flows upon you, arousing you again and again.
>
> Daniel Matt, *The Essential Kabbalah*

This of course I associated with the spontaneous prose and freestyle I'd been practicing. The same warm feeling and new understanding I'd find in these practices went beyond, for me, what Western psychologists consider when they are tapping the unconscious or subconscious. I felt ecstatic while writing improvisationally on paper or combining letters and words orally, off the top. I studied in Swansea, Wales, for a semester and went for long walks along cliffs near the Atlantic Ocean in open, green pastures surrounded by sheep. I'd freestyle, have spontaneous conversations with the universe. One day I came into a cluster of trees, closed my eyes, and began rhyming. It was as if the birds heard and started layering their voices beneath mine, as if we were communicating and creating together. The wind wove through trees like a rhythm track. I was transported to a sanctuary, found through freestyle.

There are many other experiences. Freestyle and spontaneous prose are part of my spiritual practice today. Progressively, I see more and more similarities between the orality in hip-hop and Judaism. The hazzan, for instance, tells stories to the congregation through rhythm, as does the emcee. I think of the oral historians before the Bible was codified, griots of the Hebrew people, similar to those of West Africa and all indigenous storytellers. This kind of comparative religious theorizing continues to strengthen my interest in Judaism and continues to reinforce KRS-One's claim that "Moses passed as the Pharaoh's grandson / so he had to look just like him"(*Ghetto Music: The Blue Print of Hip-Hop*, Boogie Down Productions, 1989, "Why Is That?").

I am delving deeper into both traditions, to access the richness of each and see how they connect and work simultaneously within me. Judaism wishes to make the profane sacred via numerous mindful daily practices, including kosher laws and the wearing of the yarmulke. Hip-hop makes the profane funky, turns the discarded, forgotten elements of dominant culture into subversive creation; the invisibility of urban centers where people of color live become immediately visible, a kid's name scrawled on public transit. Each wishes to transform the present into a timeless now.

Hip-hop utilizes sampling, a series of collaged sound artifacts found on old records, similarly to the way Judaism is self-referential in its use of Mishnah and Talmud. Both bring older, prerecorded sources present (Torah in Judaism and the history of black music, particularly but not limited to, in hip-hop). These sources inflect the contemporary meaning of the user, though the origin is ancient (or at least older). When rabbis invoke Torah from the bema, they contextualize the meaning to pertain to our present particularities; though Moses lived thousands of years ago, we still learn from his organizing and courage. When Pharcyde samples Donald Byrd or Jimi Hendrix (*Bizarre Ride II: The Pharcyde,* Pharcyde, 1992), we can be transported to a time or genre of music history reconfigured through the collaged sonic orchestrations of hip-hop, thereby making a commentary that is current, yet rooted in tradition. Both hip-hop sampling (and Kool Herc's advent of the break beat) and Jewish Talmud and Mishnah erase the lines between then and now. All come present, the Bible at our minyan, James Brown in our cipher, to make now sacred and historic and funky and fresh. The discussion is continuous, across generations, taking place in an absence of time: outside of history, yet firmly planted in it.

I am formulating my answer to hip-hop's metaphysical question: What do you represent? I am realizing it lies in my father's stories of old Chicago, relatives' tales around our seder table, the inspiration and teachings from Torah, the delight in the physical, in food, song, music, and theater my family has loved. The answer also lies in open mike sessions, freestyle ciphers, bombed freight trains, kids sharing tags in black books and the stories I hear in the classrooms, community and juvenile detention centers around the country and world. I not only am Jewish. I am also the illegitimate son hip-hop, the white kid who got keys to a culture that wasn't his, a culture supposed to be kept away from him. I have come full circle, full cipher, full kikel. I am a Jewish b-boy, I speak Hebonics, rock baggy pants with my head covered; I daven when I head-nod and head-nod when I daven, not one before the other, together, forever linked. I am on a path inwards to sing in words of Hashem's praises and record the misgivings and blessed multiplicities of the planet's children. I try to meet up with Shekinah every Friday night, right before a cipher jumps off. It's discipline, kind of like writing rhymes and maintaining tradition, knowhutimean?!—challah!

From Mourning to Light

LESLIE GABRIEL MEZEI

M Y GRATITUDE IS UNBOUNDED at the fullness of life, at the gift of family and friends and of the spirit. I give thanks for the rapidly growing community of those who are making this new century become one of forgiveness and reconciliation, after all the terrible atrocities we have committed against one another. I can accept and participate in all the spiritual and religious traditions of humankind. At the base of them is our awe at the miracle of existence, of creation, of our lives—and the mystery of the infinite divine spirit that we call by different names, though we cannot comprehend but can come to experience by a combination of our meager efforts and the pure gift of divine grace. With it goes a faith in the ultimate goodness of the universe.

I too have been learning to cultivate a spiritual life in the midst of the world: jobs and family responsibilities, war and peace, sickness and health, death and birth—and rebirth. My optimism for the world and its people comes from the fact that I am not unique. Many of us have come out of black tragedies to an inner light. People are daily coping with extreme vicissitudes of life, yet they survive, grow, and help each other. I am just one witness to the light glowing in all of us. May this story help you see the value of your own life, the hope in your own being, and the gratitude in the abundance of this life we all share as integral members of a profound unity in a rich diversity.

BEGINNINGS

I was born in 1931, in the time before World War II, to one of seventy Jewish families in a Hungarian town of ten thousand people. From the earliest time I remember the other kids yelling "Dirty Jew" at us. The first four years of my schooling were in a one-room school conducted by the cantor of the synagogue. Then my brother Louis and I entered a high school where we were the only Jews. We could attend classes but were barred from all other activities. One winter day the whole school, some two hundred students, surrounded us and pelted us with snowballs. Finally, Louis started crying and we ran inside.

Our saving grace was the parks and forests surrounding our dusty town. We picked violets in the spring and small wild strawberries in the summer; we tobogganed in inadequate clothing in the winter. Once I ran across the road and fell down in front of a horse-drawn sled. The curved front end of one of the runners was right over my head when the driver brought the horse to a stop. Was my guardian angel, Gabriel, there?

We went to synagogue on the weekends, but did not have an observant household, nor did we get to experience the joys of the Sabbath and the holidays. Our religious education was primitive—I still struggle with the image of the huge angry bearded man sitting on a throne in the sky. My ongoing ethical dilemma was this: is it better to read a few words of Hebrew correctly, then skip some to catch up, or to keep up with the others by moving my body and chanting, without the words? It was a lifelong struggle, choosing more and more the attunement, the feeling, the intention, and less the form, the content, the precision. We were embedded in, and excluded from, a Christian milieu: the wonderful processions with colored statues of Jesus on the cross, mysterious chanting and singing, the candy necklaces that the children could eat one by one. Across the street from us was a large cemetery. The night of All Saints' Day there were candles on every grave, creating a magical illumination.

THE CATASTROPHE

We were very poor. Even though my father was a lawyer, he worked for the local farmers, who could give him little for his assistance. Then the German army took over (it took two full days for their armored column to pass our town), and a brutal Nazi government was installed. My father could no longer practice at all. He was a kind man and well liked, so in March 1944, when I was twelve, he was warned that they would take all the Jews away from the countryside. We fled by train to the capital, Budapest, some twenty kilometers away. But the truck with our poor belongings was stopped at the border. My father went back to get it released and to help the others. Instead, he was taken to Auschwitz and killed in the gas chambers. By that time my older brother, Paul, was in the Ukraine in a forced labor camp. Soon after, my sister Klari was taken to a concentration camp.

And I was having the time of my life! My first cousin—she was the same age as I—took me all over the magical city with its palaces, cathedrals, parks, playgrounds, the noise of the cars and streetcars, the smell of the street vendor's food and flowers. But then they began to take Jews away from the city too. Once we were in the lineup to be taken to the Danube and shot, but my older sister, Miriam, somehow talked them into letting us go back to our apartment. I had just turned thirteen and had my bar mitzvah there, in a rabbi's study. I remember the chant to this day, but I had no idea what I was reading or why.

Then we had to move to an apartment house that was under the protection of Raul Wallenberg, the Swedish diplomat. After a few weeks they started taking people away from there too, so we went on to the next place, where Wallenberg gave us Swedish passports. Thus were many of us saved by a man who disappeared in the Soviet Union after the war and was never heard from again. I feel proud that Canada, my country for fifty five years now, has made him its first honorary citizen.

When the ghetto was about to be closed off, my sister Miriam and I walked out, and told the authorities that we were refugees from the country and lost everything, including our papers—and, of course, she said, we weren't Jewish. We were given ration coupons and the apartment of a Jewish family; the table was still set from their last interrupted meal. I went back into the ghetto alone to get the rest of the family and had to walk by a storefront that was piled to the ceiling with corpses. My mother, my brother Louis, and Miriam's three-year-old son, Adam, then came out with me to join Miriam in the apartment. It was toward the end of the siege of Budapest by the Russians, and we had to spend most of the time in the cellar, together with some Hungarian and even German soldiers. We were terrified that young Adam, the son of an Orthodox Jew (who perished in a labor camp) would blurt out something that would give us away. We were also terrified of the constant explosions. On the day we were to be liberated, I had just gone up to the toilet at ground level when I was deafened by a terrible crash. A shell exploded just where I had passed a few seconds before. Was Gabriel there again?

SURVIVORS

After liberation my sister Klari (literally skin and bones) and brother Paul returned, and we all went to the displaced persons camps in southern Germany. For a while we were being trained to be farmers in a kibbutz (cooperative community) in Palestine. Then Paul applied for us boys to go to the United States, to get an education and make something of ourselves. But my mother and sister Klari were going on the illegal ship *Exodus '47*, and Louis decided that we would go too. As the youngest, I didn't make the decisions, and was thus sheltered from having to know the full consequences.

We left Marseilles, France, on my sixteenth birthday and reached Haifa harbor. After a brief battle we were shipped back to Europe on three British prison ships. We had maggoty biscuits to eat and some soup, and we staged hunger strikes. But we would dance the hora (Jewish circle dance) for hours. We were finally forced off the boats and put into a camp in Germany, reminiscent of the Nazi concentration camps. The propaganda value of our rough treatment was a great help to the establishment of the State of Israel by the United Nations soon afterward.

NEW LIFE

By the time we returned, we had missed our chance to go to the United States, and that's how I became a Canadian, taken in as a war orphan by a Jewish family in Montreal. My mother and sisters went to Israel and all lived to a ripe old age. Klari, the camp survivor, was the last of my siblings to go. She died just this past year.

After five years I moved to Toronto and married Annie, a survivor from Poland, who was often hidden in a hole dug under a farm kitchen. We had two children. Annie trained as a social worker, and I started working with computers in 1954 and eventually taught computer science and did research in computer graphics at the University of Toronto.

WE ARE TESTED

But then our peaceful world collapsed. After fifteen years of our marriage, Annie developed a brain tumor. It took nine years of struggle, three operations, and many rounds of radiation and chemical treatments before she succumbed in 1977. I had to look after the family and could not afford to collapse from this shattering blow. And I needed to face the fact that she would die, that our very existence as a couple would be no more. Sometimes Annie would say to me, "I am mourning for myself."

We had the support of family, although I was the one to try to keep them all on an even keel, but we did not have the support of a faith community. We had rejected the religion for which we had suffered so much, since we weren't taught a real appreciation of its value. I began to read about psychology, religion, and spirituality, and gradually I found help from the various faith traditions: from Christianity, for example, that we all have our cross to bear and are given the strength to bear it;

from Buddhism, that we all have the Buddha-nature—we just have to learn how to access it. My nephew sent me a book from Israel about a rabbi who felt that any day when he could not help someone was a wasted day; he taught me the satisfaction of being of service to others. I was being forced to begin to know myself.

I talked to a God I didn't think I believed in. As Annie was lying in a coma in early 1977, I wished that she would let go—then, feeling guilty, I bargained that I should die rather than her. I was losing the acceptance of our situation that I thought I had achieved. Then, as I was driving on the Don Valley Parkway one early Sunday morning, a Bach cantata playing on the radio, I suddenly said, "I give up. I surrender. Let happen what will, I will accept it. I will stop this struggle." And I felt a release, a sudden joy, followed by a feeling of peace that stayed with me, that gave me patience to sit quietly with Annie until the last night before she passed on. It also allowed me to give the eulogy at her funeral:

> I am at peace with what has to be—even though it is not given to us to know why. I am no longer sorry for her, I am no longer sorry for myself, I am no longer sorry for you—her family, friends, and admirers—for we were all enriched by having known her.

Then I could enter a period of mourning, of grief work, not only for her but for my father, my mother, and all the others. I felt open to the world, patient, accepting whatever would come. I particularly remember a trip to Israel, sitting under a starlit sky by the campfire of a new community in the desert, as the Arab watchmen were roasting a lamb and making pita bread for the new settlers, and I felt they were my brothers.

NEW START

A year later I was married again, to Kathy, a seventh-generation Canadian, with five children between us. I didn't believe that I could love again, and be loved, but it happened. In our twenty-five years together, we have had the full range of joys and tribulations of a large

family, able to be a support to each other. And now, I am about to embark on the next adventure: I will accompany my daughter Frances to
south China to an orphanage from which she will adopt a little girl,
who will become our ninth grandchild.

In 1978, I took a two-year leave of absence and then left the univer-
sity, continuing the spiritual search on which I was launched. The
Association of Humanistic Psychology conferences offered all sorts of
New Age groups, as well as practitioners of ancient spiritual techniques.
At midnight, on the grass of the Princeton University campus, some
Sufi drummers and singers started their chant, and I found myself
slowly whirling round and round, and the world and its cares fell away.
There was no mental chatter, only the whirling and my spirit lifting.
Time stopped. I must have gone on the better part of two hours, spon-
taneously, with no previous experience of this spiritual practice.

Another highlight was singing and dancing with the late Rabbi
Shlomo Carlebach most of one night, at a Jewish *Ruach* (Spirit) retreat
at Woodstock, New York, in a Zen Buddhist Center, which used to be
a Christian monastery. Here is an excerpt of a poem that came to me,
in the style of Shlomo:

> Now open your hearts and listen to me, my beautiful friends.
>
> What I want to tell you is deep, very deep; it's the inside of the
> inside of the inside....
>
> We all live with the Holocaust, I came out of it, as one of the
> Redeemed Children.
>
> I know that a Holocaust can come again. It is the blackest of the
> blackest black evil.
>
> And yet, I also know that the Lord's help can come in an instant.
>
> The Messiah may well come today, at this very moment,
>
> With the brightness of the light, of the truest light.
>
> How to live at the intersection? Between annihilation and eternal
> life?
>
> Holding the Holocaust in one hand and the Messiah in the other?

With the black void of death and the bright light of life?

Come Armageddon or the Kingdom of Heaven, we will sing and dance, we will cry and laugh,

With Shlomo and his heavenly host, to the depth of the depth of our heart.

Though we died six million deaths, and many more,

We know we have lived, we have touched heart to heart,

L'Chaim.

INTERFAITH

Soon after that, I attended my first Universal worship service. Candles were lit to all the religions, we read from their sacred books, which lay side by side, and we experienced chants from many of the traditions. I realized that I could be for all the religions without having to be against any. What a revelation! This dissolved my guilt feelings about being involved with other religions while not practicing my own. It took many more years before I could come back to a synagogue, fast on the Day of Atonement, and be able to say openly, "I am a Jew." Admittedly, I am everything else too, but at least I no longer have to deny my origins.

Then I found the additional joy of the involvement of the body in the Dances of Universal Peace, round dances to the sacred chants of many traditions. They came out of the legacy of Hazrat Inayat Khan, a great Indian musician who was sent to the West in 1910 by his spiritual teacher to unite East and West. He was the first Sufi mystic teacher in the West and founded an interfaith approach to spiritual growth, now called the Sufi Order International. Here is a message that combines the wisdom of many traditions, with roots that go back a long way, yet looking to meet the needs of the future.

I was initiated into this path in 1984. It was a relief to have my own spiritual home, not to be constantly searching for a way. For the next ten years I opened myself to many teachers. I would spend much of my time at weekend retreats crying inwardly. The spiral of mourning and acceptance needed to continue, at different levels. On one silent retreat, in my reverie Inayat Khan appeared to me and said: "Your way is not the way of comfort. You will have to find your own path." This lesson has guided me ever since. I have many teachers, but I have to feel my own way along the path.

About ten years ago it became clear that it was time to give something back. I took training in the Universal worship service, and was ordained a *cherag,* enabling me to conduct the services. We have had a monthly public worship service in Toronto ever since, and I am often asked to demonstrate it to high school classes in world religion.

I have retired from the personal-financial-planning profession, in which I was engaged after I left the university, and am now involved full-time in the rich interfaith activities in our area. There are various dialogue groups and many other events, involving representatives of all faith traditions. I edit an e-mail newsletter, which goes to over four hundred people, about the interfaith events and resources in our area and internationally (interfaithunity@cs.com). I have been enriched by the friendship of a large number of colleagues who are steeped in their own faiths, but respect everyone else's and even participate in one another's worship. For me that has become the greatest joy: to sit at a Sikh *gurdvara* and absorb their worshipful chanting; to pray with Muslims shoulder to shoulder; to meditate with Buddhist monks and in Hindu temples; to take communion (where I am allowed) with Christians; to partake in a sweat lodge ceremony with our aboriginal spiritual leaders (I was once given a sacred eagle's feather); to chant *"la illaha il'allah"* (there is no God but the One God; there is nothing but the Divine) in the Sufi *zikher* (circle of remembrance); and to attend a variety of Jewish places of worship. My cup runneth over.

FORGIVENESS

Four years ago I participated in a spiritual care course offered at the Abode of the Message. We met for four weekends in that lovely hilly setting, with a natural pond, and forests like those of my childhood. A large part of the program involved self-examination. Once again, I revisited my past, what I have lost, and what I have gained. Again I got closer to accepting and even liking myself and my life. There was only one more step to finally overcome the underlying anxiety that still haunted me.

Through a remarkable set of circumstances I found myself in Krakow, the old imperial capital of Poland, and got a driver to take me to the nearby concentration camp, Auschwitz. There I joined a group on a three-hour tour showing us all the chilling details. There was a freezing wind, which chilled me even further, thinking of the prisoners standing outside for hours with practically no clothing. Finally, we got to Berkenau, the second camp to which, late in the war, the train tracks took the Hungarians, like my father, directly to the gas chambers and crematoria. I wanted to touch my father's spirit and let it go, and I did. I have been much less obsessed and anxious about it since. Then I wanted to touch the spirits of the other victims and let them go, and I did. But I also found myself wanting to touch the spirits of the victimizers, the Nazis, and I did. Something in me urged me to forgive them. And I did. And now I am glad that I could.

EPILOGUE

The phrase "the acceptance that surpasses all understanding" kept going through my head at the Abrahamic Reunion at the Abode of the Message in early December, 2003. And the most miraculous part was that I could accept that warm acceptance of my sisters and brothers: Jews, Christians, and Muslims. I came primarily to hear Brother Wayne Teasdale. I have been so taken by his concept of interspirituality that I have been giving his book *The Mystic Heart* to friends. I was relating this to him in the meditation hall of this once Shaker community in New Lebanon, New York, now the hub of the Sufi Order International in North America. I told him a little of my story of coming out of the blackness of the Holocaust to this unifying interfaith work, and the inclusive Universal worship service. He said, "Leslie, I am coediting a book of stories of transformation, and I want your story in it. Can you give me seven pages by Christmas?" It was just the impetus I needed. People have long been suggesting that I publish my story.

Sustaining a Commitment to the Common Good

Jim Keen

M Y MOTHER WAS A QUAKER who grew up in the strongly Quaker environment of Richmond, Indiana. She married my father, a young architect of Pennsylvania Dutch and Swedish lineage, a couple of weeks before the market crash of 1929. My father's family, though descended in part from Anabaptists, had settled comfortably into Methodism. My father, weary of his own childhood diet of fire and brimstone, was not much interested in religion, though he didn't resist my mother's inclination toward spiritual nurturance for her children.

My earliest memories regarding religion and spirituality concern my mother's lessons. My favorite childhood story was the Spanish tale of Ferdinand the Bull. Ferdinand was a placid soul who loved to sit under the cork tree and smell the flowers. Through a fit of observed ferocity when stung on the nose by a bee, Ferdinand ended up in a bull ring, where, attracted by lovely flowers worn on the hats of women spectators, he sat down, raised his nose in the air, and refused to be goaded into fighting. "Jimmy," my mother would say to me, "you can be like Ferdinand. You can sit under a tree and find God there. You should always behave yourself so people don't get the wrong impression about you, and you should never let anyone goad you into fighting." I later understood that these and other similar encounters were my mother's way of communicating her view of Quakerism to me.

Quakers in Harrisburg were few in the late 1940s, and the very small meeting met at a YMCA several miles from our home. By the time I entered the family, my parents had settled on a neighborhood church that practiced a Protestantism they each found congenial, which became the United Church of Christ. My mother thought, I later found, that Reverend Billman would have made an excellent Quaker, and thus it became my church until my early teen years, when the good minister retired at just the time when the Quaker meeting was blossoming and building Harrisburg's first meeting house. By that time my siblings were gone from the nest, and we began a transition to the Quaker meeting.

About the time I was fifteen, this transition was complicated, as I was identified as possessing some talent as a singer. The minister of music at the Presbyterian church of downtown Harrisburg approached my family, and I was offered weekly singing lessons in return for singing in the choir. Thus began my two years of sitting weekly through Presbyterian services.

After two years of Presbyterian liturgy, I spent my senior year of high school as a well-paid soloist for the leading Lutheran church in town, learning yet another liturgy. I have a strong feeling that my interest in interfaith dialogue stems from this era in my life, because at the same time I was becoming familiar with the differences in theological interpretation in several settings. I also became engaged in the social networks of the churches through my friendship with other teenaged singers, most of whom were more homegrown than I. We had many conversations about religion.

It was clear to me as early as fifteen that I wanted to attend Haverford College, mostly because its Quaker tradition fit my preferred religious identity. I had also been mulling the question of conscientious objection for several years prior to college. Continued soul searching led me as a sophomore into Edwin Bronner's class on the history and principles of Quakerism. This class featured lectures by Quaker luminaries such as Henry J. Cadbury and Douglas V. Steere. In this class, I located myself as part of a tradition with which I could identify. Cadbury spoke passionately of Rufus Jones, Clarence Pickett, and the American Friends Service Committee (AFSC), and Steere told us of his ecumenical work. This was a moment in my life that has taken on increasing meaning as I've grown older. The AFSC became a model for me of the spirituality of service to humanity. Rufus Jones's work on Quaker mysticism opened a topic with which I felt immediate and deep resonance and I trace an explicit interest in interfaith work to the inspiration of Steere's ecumenism. I also produced a paper on conscientious objection and proceeded to begin work on my own CO application in the wake of the class.

By the time I graduated from Haverford I had become active in the anti–Vietnam war movement. That and my postcollege job working on school reform in Philadelphia brought me into activist political contexts in Philadelphia, an array that included antiwar activists, social liberationists, and political activists in opposition to the national administration and the local mayoral candidate, Frank Rizzo, as well as my first acquaintance with gay activists, Black Panthers, and Gray Panthers. The years were 1967 through 1972. Need I say more? I remain rather obsessed by politics, but probably more importantly I encountered great diversity during those years. For example, I often found myself in the company of African Americans in living and social arrangements, and I spent a lot of my time crossing borders of race, class, and gender. It is from this era of my life in particular that I trace my commitment to working for a common good inclusive of the whole human family. Friendships and alliances across these borders have continued as a theme in my life and in my work.

Another watershed moment came in 1971 when a former acquaintance of mine, who had lost himself in substance abuse, walked, transformed and glowing, into an Indian restaurant where I was eating. We sat and talked, and he invited me to join him at a lecture he was about to deliver in his work as the representative of the International Meditation Society on the University of Pennsylvania campus. After his lecture I decided to give meditation a try. If it was responsible for the change I observed in him, it might work in some good way for anyone. The instant I was initiated, I felt an extraordinary energy course from my forehead across the top of my head and down my back. My first thought was of myself as a baby in my crib, with this very mantra repeating inside of me. I remember thinking, oh, I was born knowing how to do this, and I've simply forgotten. What a joyful experience! If the course of Haverford had been a semester of coming to myself, this was an instant and visceral homecoming.

Within a few months of meditating, I'd decided to quit my job, to take a year off by saving every penny and collecting my retirement, and to apply to graduate school. I also quit smoking and began a transition from my postcollege style of life. That year culminated in my acceptance for graduate work at Harvard while I was spending time in an advanced meditation course in Maharishi's ashram, then located in Spain. The deep meditations marked a third instance of coming to myself while experiencing more intimately the existential field of being. Meditation had now become a way of life, and I decided that when I arrived at Harvard I would rededicate myself to Quakerism and seek a more direct experience of the mysticism Rufus Jones had described. Now, at twenty-seven, I felt ready to engage that dimension.

It seemed to work. My journey to the East had brought me back to my own Western mystical tradition. From that point, imminent mysticism became my pathway. I've been nurtured along the way by many Quakers in whom I've discovered reflections of mystical practice. David McClelland and Daisy Newman are among the better known, but there have been many more.

In the 1980s and 1990s, I explored esoteric mysticism with a group that was working to achieve group enlightenment through the pathway to service. My immense admiration for their work drew me to them at the beginning, and over time I understood more clearly what they intended. Regarding enlightenment, I'm open to the possibility, but my Quaker sensibilities tell me that it's more likely to occur as an indirect outcome of how we engage the world than as a direct, culminating goal for which to quest.

Let me rewind my narrative back to the time of my graduate studies at Harvard. Within a few weeks, I met the woman who was to share my journey for these past thirty years. She asked me to help with her project of organizing members of the Harvard faculty to initiate a peace studies program for undergraduates. Kenneth and Elise Boulding, another Quaker couple, had suggested this project to Cheryl when she met them the previous summer. The Bouldings believed that if Harvard had a peace studies program, other undergraduate institutions would follow, as some have. Four other students whom Cheryl recruited joined us in this project. One of these was a noted civil rights activist, Bernard Lafayette, then in his final year of graduate studies. He introduced us to another civil rights leader, Walter Leonard, who took our cause to the university's president. Derek Bok became a quiet supporter and helped with a series of modest but critical grants out of his venture fund.

The project was successful. Cheryl ran its small office and advised students, while I worked with several faculty members to create new courses, for which I served as head teaching fellow. A new venture came to us a couple of years later when we were invited to work on a report to the Club of Rome, *No Limits to Learning*, published in 1979. That work initiated our international involvement and dovetailed with our peace studies work, as both were dedicated to addressing an emerging global reality in terms intended to address human problems. When the founder of the Club of Rome proposed a new organization for young scholars and leaders to pursue the goals stated in *No Limits to Learning*, Cheryl and I joined in 1981 with a young Harvard professor, Sharon Parks, to frame a proposal to study how exemplary people develop and sustain commitments to working on the common good, defined to include the diversity of the whole human family. I was interested in an issue I'd worked on for my doctorate: how people mediate successfully between macro perspectives and micro realities—a concern that brought the liberationist perspective of peace studies together with the Club of Rome's concern for global problems.

The new initiative by the Club of Rome never fully materialized, but we undertook the research and carried it forward as an act of faith, joined along the way by Larry Daloz, until we finally found significant financial support from the Lilly Endowment in 1989. The book *Common Fire* relates to this reflection in numerous ways. First, it can be read as a road map for the spirituality of service. Reviewer Dan Goleman called it "a guidebook for the soul." Second, it was an act of service for the authors, especially through the better part of a decade of having potential funders tell us the question was too big for them. We proceeded anyway, following a shared calling rather than a conventional pathway to success. Many people tell us now that they have found the book very helpful, which warms our souls.

Since 1997, in the current phase of my life and work, the spirituality of service has led me back into teaching peace studies, serving as a researcher and evaluator for several interfaith projects, and stepping up my efforts to promote interfaith encounters as a pathway to embracing the whole human family, and to make a place for both interfaith collaboration and spiritual seeking in higher education (more about this later) as well as into collaboration with several groups who are working to generate useful, accessible tools for engaging complexity.

I'm currently doing some of the complexity work as a member of the committee that oversees the Quaker United Nations office. I'm working with several groups in Europe, as well, on the issue of engaging complexity. For me this is not simply an intellectual exercise. Rather, I feel certain that this work needs to be done for the sake of the planet, so it is for me an instance of the spirituality of service.

Likewise, in the area of service, I've volunteered my time by joining with several participants with whom I was involved in a Fetzer Institute project to form the Initiative for Authenticity and Spirituality in Higher Education (IASHE). Our efforts to place spirituality on the higher education agenda have borne fruit. We've now had an impact on most of the major associations of higher education. Members Sandy and Lena Astin and Art Chickering often draw this theme into keynote speeches, while Cynthia Johnson and I have hosted numerous panel presentations on the topic. The Astins have just completed the first major survey on student spirituality in higher education, which marks a real step forward in this effort. Recently IASHE has formed a coalition with two other groups, one of which, Education as Transformation (EasT), I serve as vice president. EasT has worked over the past decade to reframe campus ministries into places of interfaith collaboration and dialogue. EasT seeks to engage the increasing religious diversity in the American student population as an asset to twenty-first-century learning while also attempting to open space for explicit spiritual seeking that may not fit neatly into religious frameworks. I work with both of these organizations as a volunteer, as I feel called to engage in these efforts as part of my own pathway of service.

In drawing to a close, I am left with questions. Does my teenage cascade through Protestant churches underlie my interest in interfaith collaboration, or does that interest stem more from my later encounters with diversity? Perhaps a bit of both, along with other historical contingencies in my life. Has more than thirty years of meditating had an effect on my life? I certainly hope so. Am I truly a spiritual person? I feel as though I am on a spiritual path, but a good distance from catching the horizon.

Watching the Previews

BRIAN STURGULEWSKI

I T SOMETIMES SEEMS that my nose itches only when I meditate. Somehow, contemplation has a direct effect on the sensitivity of my little snout, and the moment I close my eyes the impulse to scratch it arises. This somewhat annoying phenomenon is one of a handful of difficulties I've struggled with since I began cultivating my spiritual life through meditation. Ringing phones, my affinity to doze off, and the need to "just check what's on" have, at times, made meditative relaxation quite a taxing activity. Despite the hindrances, meditation and my embracing of other religious traditions have helped me (even if they didn't stop my nose from itching) to grow in both my spirituality and my love of humanity.

I do not pretend to be perfectly mature in my spiritual life. Although I've traveled a great spiritual distance, I know that the steps I've taken are only a fraction of an infinite path that I must continue to tread. If these few lines are the prologue to my spiritual journey, then what they should more justifiably be called is a prologue to a prologue. In my mystical voyage I have only just left port. As I sail further out, however, I realize more that the waters I float upon are boundless, and the heavenly horizon I steer toward is attainable.

Allow me to apologize in advance. I was raised a Catholic. I say this not because I'm ashamed of my faith but because there is a stigma attached to Catholicism. It seems that at one time in their lives, everyone has run into an old Catholic woman who shook a cane at them and told them they were cursed to damnation because they didn't have enough reverence for the pope, the saints, and the Virgin Mary. While this may have been both terrifying and traumatic, I assure you that all Catholics are not so aggressively closedminded (some of us don't even own canes to shake).

Growing up, I was always an altar boy (in both a literal and a figurative sense). Very much interested in my faith, I always went to mass, said my prayers, and paid attention during my catechism classes. My devotion to the church was so strong that when I was a teenager my family feared I would become a priest. (Their fears prove that if the Vatican were to lift the ban on married priests I think it would be the clergy's grandchild-hungry parents who would celebrate the loudest.)

I'm not sure where or when I discovered that there were other religions. I am tempted to say it was probably where I learned most of my life lessons: at the movies. Now some of you are probably rolling your eyes, shaking your heads, and scoffing at the idea of movies as a source of spiritual knowledge. Movies are not intended to be a dogmatic reference guide. What movies teach us are messages that are deeper, bigger, and more instinctual than the words to the "Hail Mary" or the different incarnations of Brahman. Movies, when they're good, speak not to our specific faiths but to our collective humanity. They transcend the boundaries of church and carry a mysticism that binds us all.

Though I am an ardent defender of the Catholic Church, I do believe that it has, at times, made it difficult to look beyond Catholicism and discover the beauty and truth of other faiths. This is a problem that the church must continue to work on. As a Catholic schoolboy, I didn't have many outlets for other kinds of religious information, so the mystery of a dark theater is where my spiritual flowering took bloom. Long before I knew of Buddha, Brahman, or Allah, I saw mystical messages in films like *Groundhog Day, Ikru, Star Wars,* and *Children of Heaven.* These films and their stories inspired me, opening my eyes to the mystical world around me.

As I grew I began to pester everyone with questions about other religions and their beliefs. My high school theology teacher, Mr. Raker, was a film fan himself, and we would talk in great depth about movies and the different messages they conveyed about faith, mysticism, and religion. Mr. Rakar was the first person to introduce me to meditation and to bring to my attention the spiritual and ethical depth of cinema. I grew more and more enamored of cinema and the remarkably diverse spiritual world around me.

Abandoning their fears of my becoming a priest, my family soon began to tremble at the thought of another humble occupation: filmmaker. Who's poorer than a priest who has taken a vow of poverty? A struggling filmmaker! Despite my family's concerns, the mystical messages of cinema had me entranced. As I began to write and direct, it became clear that my calling is that of a storyteller: someone who can reach the hearts and imaginations of entire audiences through the use of film.

Secure in my method, I have spent the past few years of my life sculpting and maturing my message. It is very easy to overlook the responsibility that filmmakers have. Under the guise of entertainment, the film industry has proliferated negative messages about religion, race, gender, and sexuality. It sometimes seems for every one *Kundun* made there are ten other films that carry poor messages to misguided audiences. This is a cycle that I hope someday to alter, and with a greater sense of mysticism and the aid of the divine presence (God, Brahman, Allah, or whatever you perceive it to be) I will accomplish this task. I've been very blessed to have the best possible spiritual guidance in the form of friends, family, and of course films.

As I said earlier, I do not pretend to be perfectly matured in my spiritual life. If my life were a movie, we would still be watching previews. Although I am more greenhorn than guru, as I grow and mature as a filmmaker and a mystic my heart continues to open (hopefully my nose will cease to itch), and one message rings within me like a mantra in my soul. Be open—not just to the mysticism in other faiths but also to the mysticism in our own lives and work. Be open to the Divine in our own pursuits, for it will sustain us. Most importantly, be aware of the mysticism in our lives, for it will give them meaning.

The Yellow Carnation

IDA-REGINA LUCAS OLIVER

I WAS BORN AND RAISED in a Jewish family. My maternal grandfather was from the line of high priests, and my paternal grandfather was Orthodox. My immediate family was somewhere between Conservative and Reform. As a child, I was fascinated by the picture of Jesus with the big red heart hanging in our neighbor's apartment and the Jesus movies on television at Christmas and Easter. However, my family cautioned me against believing in Jesus.

For as long as I can remember, I felt that something was missing from my life. I felt as if I had a hole in my soul. As a young adult, I became interested in Buddhism and Hinduism. Then I joined a Unitarian church. I searched for the answer in books and relationships, but nothing filled the void that I sensed. I prayed to God, "Please send me someone to love who will love me back!"

Not long afterward, I met a man whom I thought was the answer to my prayer. But the relationship ended badly, and I became despondent. I thought I had done something to ruin the relationship that I believed God had sent me. Ashamed, I felt that I could no longer turn to God. Then, some Catholic friends explained the story of the Prodigal Son to me. They told me about God's love and said that I needed God especially now.

One night, I called a friend and asked her if she believed in Jesus.

She said that she did. I asked her to tell me about him. As I fell asleep that night I felt as if something like a mist was moving through me. Then I heard myself saying, "Jesus is my Savior, Jesus is my Savior." When I woke up in the morning I knew that I was supposed to be baptized.

I talked with a priest serving as a chaplain at the hospital where I was doing research. I told him that I wanted to be baptized. He said that I needed to go through classes first. I told him that this was not between a church and me, but between God and me. I think that he would have done it, but I did not want him to get in trouble. However, the sense that I was supposed to be baptized was very strong within me. Therefore, I asked a Lutheran friend of mine if his pastor would baptize me. (I knew the pastor because I had gone to Christmas Eve services with my friend and his family for several years.) The pastor agreed to baptize me on the following Saturday afternoon.

On Friday, I went to a bookstore and looked at the books, thinking about the scheduled baptism. I started to get upset. What if I was making a mistake? Was I being a traitor to my Jewish heritage? I remembered my mother telling me that we did not need any middlemen; we could go to God directly. I decided to cancel the baptism.

On my way home, a man with long dark hair and a beard approached my car at a stoplight. He was carrying a box of carnations, and he motioned to me with the yellow one he held. I told him that I did not want to buy any flowers. He said, "This is not for sale; it is a gift. It is free." I repeated that I did not want to buy any flowers. He repeated, "This is not for sale; it is a gift. It is free." I took the flower.

I drove away and felt as if something had punched me in the chest. I thought, "Long hair and a beard! How many people denied Jesus?" I decided that the flower would be a sign of a covenant between God and me. I would put it on the church altar when I was baptized.

The next day, as I drove to the baptism, I still had some concern about betraying my Jewish heritage. I asked God to make the rain stop and the sun to shine for even a moment as a sign that I was doing the right thing. But it continued to rain.

In his office at the church, the pastor asked me questions about what I believed. I told him that I believed I was supposed to be baptized. My friend, who was an elder in the church, said that he thought that I was acting in good faith, so they decided to go ahead with the baptism.

As we walked toward the sanctuary, I asked them if I could put the carnation on the altar. When I approached the altar, I saw that an arrangement of yellow carnations was already there. The arrangement was symmetrical, except that there was a hole where one of the flowers was missing. My carnation fit into the space.

It was still raining when I left the church after my baptism. All of a sudden, the rain stopped, the clouds opened for a moment, and I saw the sun. Then the clouds closed, and the rain started again.

God makes better plans than we do. When I prayed "Please send me someone to love who will love me back," I wanted a boyfriend. But God knew that I needed a different kind of relationship first and answered that prayer by sending me Jesus. Since then, my life has been transformed.

About a year after I was baptized, I experienced an inescapable sense that God was calling me to do something. In 1990, I enrolled in a clinical pastoral education program at a hospital. During that time, God also answered my prayer by sending my husband, Ken. He is a devoted Christian whose ministry is advocating and educating for affordable housing policy. Ken and I agree that loving and serving God is our first priority and commitment.

My clinical pastoral education supervisors encouraged me to go to seminary. I received my master of divinity degree from North Park Theological Seminary in Chicago in 1998. The Evangelical Covenant Church ordained me as a minister in 2001 and the Association of Professional Chaplains granted me board-certified chaplain status in 2003. Currently, I serve as staff chaplain and coordinator of the department of pastoral care and healing arts at Glenbrook Hospital (Evanston Northwestern Healthcare) in Glenview, Illinois, and as one of the adjunct faculty at North Park Theological Seminary. I am also training as a spiritual companion at the Institute of Spiritual Companionship in

Chicago.

As I learned more about being a Christian, the spiritual significance of my experiences that baptismal weekend in 1988 became clearer to me. The day I met the man with the yellow carnation was Good Friday. His gift was not for sale; it was free.

The Secret of the Six Perfections and the Four Immeasurable Minds

MARTHA HOWARD, MD

I WAS RAISED A METHODIST IN IOWA. I went to Sunday School and church, and, as I grew up, sang in the choir and attended the Methodist Youth Fellowship (MYF). I prayed, memorized Bible verses, and went to church camp. I wanted desperately to feel connected with the greatness and the love that were always attributed to God. Somehow I kept running into my own skepticism, which began, oddly enough, when I was less than four years old. I remember being in Sunday school and looking down at my high-top white shoes as I listened to the story of Jonah and the whale. I came home and questioned my mother: "You know those fairy tales we read sometimes—are they true?" And my mother said, "No, of course not, they're just stories." Then I asked, "Well, what about the Bible stories, like Jonah and the whale? Are they true?" "Yes, of course," she said. "They are from the Bible."

That explanation didn't make sense to me even at my young age. This was in the mid-1940s, long before the beginning of the scientific study of miracles that we have today, so I had nothing to convince me. I was left with my doubts and with my critical eye as a young adult, witnessing (in my teachers at Sunday School and the adults around me) too much piety on Sunday that was not backed up by real day-to-day virtue during the week. Maybe one of the problems was that by chance my Sunday School teacher/MYF advisor was also the boss in my after-school job at a real estate company during the week.

At that same time I sometimes went to church with a friend's family, who were Presbyterians. There didn't seem to be a bit of difference between their church and mine. I made some visits to Lutherans and Baptists and saw no evidence (in that same skeptical, critical mind of mine) for any difference between them. I couldn't figure out how it was that they seemed so intent on being in their little groups, even making disparaging or competitive remarks about the other churches, when to my mind, all of those Protestant denominations in my hometown could not have been more alike if they had tried.

In any case, there was nothing to hold me into the religious orientation of my youth. I admired the life of Jesus and the example he set in the way he lived his life. But, to my way of thinking at the time, I didn't see anyone who called himself or herself Christian trying very hard to follow Jesus's example.

To me, as an idealistic young adult, it was all a lot of talk. By the time I entered college, I attended the Unitarian church off and on, but I thought that the whole enterprise of religion was pretty much irrelevant at best and harmful and divisive at worst, and did not want much to do with it. I didn't think it made people act any better. As a matter of fact, my feeling at the time was that religion made people act much more hatefully toward one another. As I read about historical events like the Inquisition and the Salem witch trials, I began to think of religious leadership as having a primary interest in dominating other people's minds and lives in order to sway them to their own version of "the truth" (whatever they thought that was), or to gain wealth and power. They did not seem to be focused on being an influence for good in the world, or in leading their own lives in a way that resembled, in any form, the kinds of lives that were lived by the great spiritual masters of all the faiths.

I began to study Buddhism, Confucianism, and Taoism as a require-ment in graduate school. I remember thinking how wonderful it must have been that somehow people were able to combine these beliefs in China, that they were able to exist side by side and complement one another. Of course, in my young, idealistic way, I did not understand some of the sectarian battles within and between them because it was all so academic and far away. I was attracted to Taoism and Buddhism. I thought of them more as something very remote that could be studied, but I did not really see how they could be practiced, here in the United States, in the present day.

I left graduate school, had two wonderful children, and went to medical school at the age of thirty-eight. I was so immersed in what I was doing that there was no time to think. I passed through that time as if I were on another planet, in another orbit, out of time.

During this time my parents, who had always been devout Methodists, left their church. They were offended by a series of new ministers and the amount of "hellfire and brimstone" that had been coming from the pulpit. They had always seen the role of a minister as being an educator and a leader, encouraging people in the congregation to live better lives, especially by the example of the minister's own life. My mother had always said, "You can be close to the Divine anywhere, especially in the beauties of nature; you don't have to be in church." In their later lives, that is what my parents did. I believe it is the example of their sincere attempt to live their own lives as true Christians that allowed me to find my own spiritual path, though it was not to be pri-marily as a Christian.

I was shocked to find that at the end of medical school, residency, and a tour of duty in the Public Health Service, it was 1989, I was forty-eight years old, and I was ill. I was assisting at a cesarean section at 5 a.m., after being up all day and the previous night. I felt faint and "scrubbed out" of the procedure. I didn't make it out of the operating room but collapsed at the end of the table. I had a heart problem but refused to stay in the hospital. I went home, called up my friend who is a practitioner of traditional Chinese medicine and asked him for some Chinese herbs. A dear friend, who was staying with me at the time while she went to art school and her daughter went to high school, half humorously threatened that if I didn't quit work she would lock me out of the house. At the end of the week, I left work.

About three weeks after that, a friend called me and said she had heard that His Holiness the Dalai Lama was going to be teaching in Madison, Wisconsin, and I *had* to go. I told her that I was too exhausted to go anywhere; that I was very sorry, but I would have to refuse her invitation. She said that it was so important, she would drive me there. I finally agreed. As it turned out, something happened that she could not drive me, but I already had the tickets, so I dragged myself into the car and drove myself. I had no idea what a Buddhist teaching was like, so I walked in, not knowing what to expect.

My heart sank as I saw the room. There were rows of wooden folding chairs, and I had not brought any cushion to sit on. I didn't know whether I was well enough to sit there for six hours a day, three days in a row. I thought I might just fall right off the chair, but I need not have worried. I was so drawn to the teaching that the chair seemed to disappear. H.H. the Dalai Lama came in, seated himself on the dais, and began to talk. I had no idea what it was going to be about, so I started taking notes—which I still have. It turned out that this was the Tibetan Buddhist Avalokiteshvara teaching, which is about dedicating oneself to learning to think, speak, and act with the compassion of an enlightened being.

I was impressed with this. I wasn't being asked to believe in something, to worship anyone, or to be evangelized. I was being asked to practice a kind of discipline of compassion and kindness in my own life, and, in terms of the sufferings of human existence, become part of the solution instead of part of the problem. This made sense to me, as did H.H. the Dalai Lama as an example and as a teacher. He actually practiced what he preached. So I set about to do my best to follow his example, which has been far more difficult and demanding than I had any idea of at the time.

To support my Buddhist practice, I have done a lot of reading and studying. In the past few years I have been studying the Lamrim teachings. These teachings begin with simple training about ways to practice an ethical mental outlook and motivation in daily life. Eventually, the teachings about meditation bring realization of the concept of the underlying nature of phenomena, which is termed emptiness. This understanding of the idea that all phenomena are "empty" of independent self-existence, and are all interdependent, impermanent, and dependent on causes and conditions for their existence, is basic to making the distinction between the way things truly are and the way we perceive them. Then the teachings lead to combining the realization of emptiness with the motivation of the bodhisattva (enlightened, compassionate being) to work with compassion and lovingkindness to benefit all beings. Finally, there is the realization of a state of full enlightenment, beyond concepts and duality.

This sounded at the beginning as if it might be too complicated. However, I was determined at least to start. I tried once, and got "wound up" in the various practices so much that I felt distracted and confused. So I did other kinds of meditation for more than two years. I went to more teachings and talked to more teachers. Then something drew me to start again.

Very seriously, I began to follow the book called *Path to Bliss: A Practical Guide to the Stages of Meditation* (Snow Lion Publications, 1991). This book is an English translation of the Lamrim teachings given at the main temple in Dharamsala, India, in 1988 by H.H. the Dalai Lama. The book could not be written more clearly, and H.H. the Dalai Lama, as usual, is a great teacher. In the book, there is a very skillful introduction and history of the teachings. Then there are some practical instructions on how to create of an environment conducive to meditation, telling the practitioner exactly what to do in order to prepare to practice. Then there are the preparatory practices, and finally the main meditations.

As I worked through the practices, prayers, and visualizations, I saw that each stage of meditation followed logically from the previous one. I began to do the preparatory practices, and then one or two of the main meditations each day. Yet, there seemed to be two things holding me back.

The first was an instruction that seemed like an "out of sight" mystery that could never be solved, something that looked like a secret so deep that I would never find the answer, the magic footnote, or the secret text in this lifetime. The assertion in the book was that there is a method that can erase all the "subtle imprints" of the three "afflictive emotions." These three emotions are known in Buddhism to be ignorance, anger, and greed. Other words for them are bewilderment, hatred, and lust, or delusion, aversion, and attachment.

These emotions are as powerful as quicksand. We know that under their influence we are capable of being sucked in—pulled down from our highest intentions. We might blurt out something we wished we hadn't said in anger when in the middle of an argument (that began, we thought, as a calm discussion). We could feel almost compelled to say something cruel to "get back" when we think we have been hurt, and to grab for what we think we want or are entitled to as we jump ahead of someone else. We are capable of turning away, ignoring or denying some problem that is happening right in front of us, and therefore failing to help.

Afflictive emotions inevitably lead us to trouble. A practitioner can work and work to decrease them, but they can still leave subtle traces: tracks that can lead right back into a life of suffering. Coming to the realization that your own responses are one of the central causes of your own suffering makes you bound, like Shakyamuni Buddha, to look for a way to free yourself and others and move toward a more enlightened way of living.

I was amazed to read in that book that there really is a method for wiping away even the subtle traces of ignorance, anger, and greed, and getting free of their grip. I imagined how wonderful it would really be to have the skill and stability to act from a center of calm and kindness, no matter what anyone else said or did, even if they intended harm toward me. I considered what the world might be like if every single human being in it acted with the kindness, compassion, joy, and stability of H.H. the Dalai Lama himself.

I thought how much better life would be with the wisdom and understanding to see deeply into a situation immediately, and simply be able either to avoid having a surge of anger or resentment or dislike come up, or at least to be able to process it immediately and refrain from speaking or acting while in the grip of a negative emotion. But I really did not think I would ever find the text that told me how to do it—at least not in this lifetime. So there I was, held back by my belief that

I might not ever find the secret method to erase those persistent, troublesome traces of ignorance, anger, and greed.

The second thing that was holding me back was my attitude toward death. My mother had died six years before, and I was taking care of my dying father. I think that in my parents' process of dying, I began to see and feel my own death. I was resigned, in a way. Death was inevitable. That was that; I had to accept it. But I did not really fully understand that resignation is not acceptance. As I worked on the teachings I kept skipping over the section about death, thinking, "I have had enough of death right now, I'll do this part later."

Then one day I decided that I had to study the death part, and I might as well do it today. I started reading, and this is what it said:

> You should develop the conviction that awareness of death and impermanence is an important element of the Buddha's teaching, and this is why the Buddha taught impermanence at the beginning of all his teachings when he first taught the Four Noble Truths. The first phase of the practice is to restrain the negative emotions.... The cause of your body is contaminated actions and delusions, and as long as you are under their influence there is no place for happiness. In a similar way there is no possibility of happiness and peace while someone is under the leadership of a very negative person. Therefore, reflect upon the fact that you are under the rule of ignorance; ignorance is like a despotic king, and anger and attachment are like his ministers. We live under the

tyranny and influence of ignorance, the self-grasping attitude, and also the self-cherishing attitude—factors that all the buddhas and bodhisattvas treat as real enemies. The worst thing is to be under the influence and grip of these negative factors....

The second phase is to engage in the method of rooting out the delusions that are the root of these negative actions. This is done by applying their opponent force, the wisdom realizing emptiness, which eliminates the grasping at self existence. Eliminating these delusions, together with their root, marks the achievement of liberation.

The third phase is to eliminate the dispositions or imprints left by the delusions that obstruct you from achieving omniscience, the direct knowledge of all phenomena. This should be done by complementing the wisdom realizing emptiness with the factors of method—compassion, bodhicitta, patience, generosity and so forth" (*Path to Bliss: A Practical Guide to the Stages of Meditation*, Snow Lion Publications, 1991, pp. 104–110).

There it was! Just what I was looking for, right in the very chapter I had been avoiding. I started to laugh and shed tears at the same time. It wasn't some kind of mysterious visualization or ritual that would eliminate those imprints of ignorance, anger, and greed! It was the daily life practice of the "four immeasurable minds": compassion, loving-kindness, sympathetic joy, and equanimity, as well as the "six perfections": generosity, morality, patience, effort, concentration, and wisdom. It was so obvious. If I wanted to get rid of the despotism, tyranny, and suffering of those afflictive emotions, the thing to do was to make my own beneficial habits of mind and action such a priority that there would be no room for anything else. It was what I had believed in all along—making the effort actually to live in the way that all spiritual teachers tell us to do. I would like to say that it was a lot easier to stay in all those good habits after that moment of truth, but often it wasn't. However, as the years go by it does get easier, and the voices of the "tyrants" are quieting down.

I really attribute any ability to continue to work on the discipline of changing my habits of thought, speech and action to the stabilizing influence of the living example of H.H. the Dalai Lama himself. It has been very important to me to find a teacher who walks his talk. I believe that it is equally important to people of all spiritual practices or religions to be able to learn by example, and it is my fervent hope that increasing numbers of leaders in all religions will take this seriously.

At one of his teachings, H.H. the Dalai Lama said that he was always happy to hear that people had been studying and practicing for any amount of time, no matter how short, but that he really began to take it seriously after it had been, say, fifteen or sixteen years of hard work. Next May will be the fifteenth anniversary of that first trip to listen to the teaching about compassion. I am glad to be "still working on it," and I count myself incredibly fortunate that somehow I made it to Madison that day.

A Christian Contemplative in an Interspiritual World

BROTHER WAYNE TEASDALE

ALL OF US ARE ON A spiritual journey of one sort or another. My path has been a progressively intermystical one as a Christian monk in a uniquely contemporary situation: an interfaith context of exploration, or what I have come to name interspirituality. In what follows I want to trace my development from my Roman Catholic roots to a Christian mystic open to the wisdom and spiritual treasures of my brothers and sisters in the other faith traditions, or who follow a different form of spirituality than mine.

I begin with my roots in Connecticut, where I was born and raised and experienced my first stirrings of the spiritual life within my Catholic environment. I move on to relate my inner state as I started college in New Hampshire, and my awakening to mysticism in earnest. I share how Thomas Keating sent me to my first interreligious conference; how Bede Griffiths invited me to come to India, and eventually to embrace *sannyāsa*, or renunciation, as a Christian monk; my first seminal meeting with His Holiness the Dalai Lama and other Tibetans; how I experienced a kind of Buddhist dark night of the soul; my integration of East and West in my own inner, contemplative consciousness; and finally where I find myself today as an interspiritual Christian mystic.

I was a pious little kid from West Hartford, Connecticut (well, pious most of the time). Catholicism was my culture, my faith, my very world. The other faiths were very remote from my experience and understanding. My anchor was Rome, especially in the pope; my hero was St. Francis of Assisi, whom I knew as a dear friend. As a child and teenager, and on into adulthood, I really must say that I knew Francis as if we had grown up together, and in a sense we did. I had read more than twenty books on the saint and on St. Clare as well, not to mention Augustine, Benedict, Teresa of Avila, John of the Cross, the Blessed Mother, and countless others.

When I was a child, nature was so magical to me, and all of life. The Divine surrounded me in the natural world with its endless wonders, in cosmos with its countless stars and galaxies, and in the mysteries of human life. An insight that has occurred to me in recent times relates to this immensely wonderful period we call childhood: a child experiences the mystical as the magical. The notion of the magical is how children process the mystical. This is one reason why *Harry Potter* is so popular with our children. When I was a child, everything to me was magical—that is, mystical.

In 1966 when I went on to St. Anselm College in New Hampshire, an extraordinary school operated by Benedictine monks, I was going through a very painful agnostic period, brought on by a confrontation with an understandably bitter Vietnam vet who was a hard-nosed atheist. It adversely affected my childlike Catholic faith. I never rejected my Catholicism but suffered through the emptiness of skepticism. I majored in philosophy to be able to confront atheism with its unquestioned assumptions, but I only discovered a more solid ground of truth when I began to have mystical experiences, which awakened me experientially to the divine reality. I have had hundreds of these experiences over the years, and they have granted me a certitude that eluded me earlier.

Of course I went on to graduate school, doing an MA in philosophy and a PhD in theology. During graduate school, Thomas Keating, a saintly Trappist spiritual master, actually my spiritual father, sent me to an East/West monastic conference to—as he put it at the time—

"baptize" me into interreligious dialogue and the whole interfaith phenomenon. It was June 1977, and prior to that I had started a correspondence with Bede Griffiths, an English Benedictine monk and spiritual writer in South India. Both Thomas Keating and Bede Griffiths have been enormously influential in my opening to other religions, particularly the traditions of the subcontinent.

I started going to India for long periods in 1986, and after my third visit in 1988, Bede invited me to accept initiation into *sannyāsa*, after sufficient spiritual preparation, I took *sannyāsa* from Father Bede on January 5, 1989. This commitment had introduced me into an Indian lineage of monastic life and contemplation, which I take very seriously. *Sannyāsa*, a medieval Sanskrit word, nevertheless names a monastic form that is at least seven thousand years old and is the origin of Hindu, Jain, and Buddhist monasticism. There have been Christian *sannyāsis* since the mid-seventeenth century, with the Jesuit priest Roberto de Nobili as the first pioneer. This is my stream of monastic tradition, combined with the Benedictine tradition of the Catholic Church in which I was previously formed, though I had never taken vows in this tradition. Whereas Thomas Keating had taught me all the principles and practices of the spiritual life, including the contemplative attitude and meditation in its form known as Centering Prayer, Bede Griffiths had schooled me in the prophetic function of speaking truth to power, and regarding the leadership of the church with a critical eye but not with any kind of hostility. I realized long ago that I have a great love for the church, but that does not mean I am silent in the face of injustice and the need for reform.

Another significant influence on my life and development, especially in relation to appreciating the other religions and the importance of the interfaith movement, is His Holiness the Dalai Lama, who has deeply inspired my life. His warmth, sanctity, wisdom, and joy have had a great impact my life and understanding. His authenticity is so intriguing to me, and I realize that in his example, Christians had a lot to learn from Buddhists, and vice versa, which is something His Holiness has often observed. His friendship is a great gift in my life.

My encounter with Buddhism, the inner processing of it, has led me into a sort of Buddhist dark night of the soul. I was caught up in its beauty, truth, and goodness and struggled to relate it to the inner beauty, truth, goodness, and mystical coherence of the Christian tradition and all my contemplative experience as a lay monk in it—a monk without a community in the usual sense: that is, a monastic family to which I belonged in a literal sense of shared life together in the same cloister. This dark night of the soul was a metaphysical anguish in my difficult task of attempting to reconcile them from within the heights and depths of my inner experience and awareness. Such a struggle can be quite overwhelming, ontologically frightening, and psychologically tentative, because it is so lonely and pioneering, introducing new realities into one's experience. Any attempt to negotiate inwardly, in an experiential way, another spiritual tradition in its deeper or esoteric truth, while reconciling it with a commitment to one's home tradition, is often psychologically traumatic in its initial disorientation, with the demands to stretch one's understanding beyond the known to the still unknown. This trauma is normal for one who remains within a home tradition and must endure the agony of uncertainty in precisely how, in my case, Buddhist and Christian mysticism come together within the cave of the heart, the inner life of contemplative experience and awareness. For me, at this point in my spiritual journey, I was trying to reconcile the utter authenticity of my experience and certitude of the Divine Reality, God, the Absolute, or Source, with the Buddhist silence on God. I have come to the realization that this issue is a lot more subtle than most might think, as well as more subtle than the ways it has been represented in the past.

Much of this Buddhist dark night of the soul I endured was a kind of shaking of my Christian foundations and a venturing out from the safe shores of the church into the mysterious, and to me hitherto un-explored, lands of the Buddha. The examples of countless Tibetans, like His Holiness the Dalai Lama; Samdhong Rinpoche, a very holy lama; Tendzin Choegyal (who is also called Ngari Rinpoche and is the Dalai Lama's younger brother); his wife, Rinchen Khando; and many other

Buddhists I know in and beyond the Tibetan Buddhist tradition, have reinforced in my understanding the utter and precious value of Buddhist spirituality as profoundly authentic.

I do feel that there is something missing for me in Buddhism, and that is its apparent lack of a tradition of seeking an ultimate source. There are many reasons for this, some of which are related to historical documentation. The sacred texts of the Buddhist tradition have had a different kind of study and commentary than the biblical criticism that we find in the Judeo-Christian tradition. Internal evidence suggests, in my view, an earlier hidden experience of the Divine in Buddhism, connected to the Buddha's experience of enlightenment and now obscured by linguistic, sociological, and historical events. Again, this whole matter is extremely subtle. In the long run, this issue of theism or nontheism will be resolved through dialogue and research. It could well be more of a linguistic or semantic question we must deal with in order to find a common ground between these two approaches.

Regardless of this and related issues, Christian and Buddhist contemplatives, along with their counterparts in Hinduism, Jainism, Judaism, Taoism, Islam, and other religious traditions; the indigenous spiritualities, including shamanism; and the enlightened ethical humanists in the scientific community, have a common ground in the mystical quest, the moral awareness, and the urgency of collaborating together on the critical issues. The most pressing and distressing of these are religiously based violence, warmongering, and ecological blindness of so many factions—individuals who simply haven't awakened to the crisis our planet is in, and the deep disparities of wealth, educational and employment opportunities, resources, and technology. The greatest work of our time is to be peacemakers, the sine qua non for stability, economic well-being for all, and the possibility of solving the environmental nightmare we are in.

I have found a sort of integration of my attempts to relate East and West in the depths and heights of my contemplative experience and understanding. I have arrived at the realization that the mystical realization, from which all the traditions of spiritual wisdom have arisen, can function as the "missing link" or bridge between the religions, as the heart of the dialogue of the world's religions. That dialogue is crucial in forging ahead in the interfaith arena.

An insight has opened up for me in the recognition of an interspiritual ground that ultimately harmonizes the seeming ontological differences, as for instance between Buddhism and Christianity, or theism and nontheism, and has the potential of connecting and uniting the religions, and people who do not belong to any specific religion, while maintaining the support, strength, and individuality of each set of beliefs.

I believe that there is a universal mystical experience, and a spirituality deriving from it, a global or planetary spirituality, but it is neither intentional nor systematic. No group got together at the dawn of human consciousness and said: "Let us create an overarching mystical wisdom and practice." Rather, interspirituality—the exploration of this common ground—is the discovery that the mystical is a universal dimension of humanity's inner life and experience. All of the contents of this dimension—the various manifestations of its precious experiences, insights, coherent visions, methods, and practices—are part of this intermystical thread of humankind's common source of spirituality. In the end, all of it will be known to reveal the Source as originating point of an ongoing revelation.

Thus, I find myself a Christian mystic in an increasingly interspiritual world threatened by the dangerous refusal by fundamentalist extremism to acknowledge the authenticity and value of other belief systems. Up the road of history this extremism will dissipate, but not through violent reactions to it. Through patient dialogue and the careful building of consensus, a way forward will emerge. Such dialogue and consensus building is the practical side of interreligious work. This work has as its long-term task the envisioning and development of a new global polity: a civilization of love; a new universal society with a *heart*, one conceived in wisdom; compassion; an ethics of kindness; and the full awakening of all humanity, as well as other sentient beings, to their ultimate potential for spiritual maturity.

I would like to close this piece with what I call the Intention Practice, an exercise I find very beneficial in locating and maintaining perspective. Here is how it goes:

> Close your eyes. Take a few deep breaths. Allow yourself to relax, for it is in relaxing that the greatest breakthroughs occur. Now rest for a few minutes in the pervading stillness and silence. Be absorbed in it. Then identify what it is you truly believe that you most want. What is the deepest, purest intention of your heart, your very being? Ask yourself: does this intention unite me with the Source? Does it benefit all beings? If it does, be devoutly grateful. If it does not, ask that your intention be enlightened, your heart expanded, your understanding widened, and your will strengthened.

Conclusion

Toward a Unified Humanity: From the Age of Materialism to the Age of Integral Spirituality

Brother Wayne Teasdale and Martha Howard, MD

ALL OF THE STORIES in this volume indicate that something important is stirring in the depths of humankind. Bede Griffiths, one of the great prophetic figures of the twentieth century, used to proclaim, on numerous occasions and in various contexts: "We are entering a new age!" These stories suggest, among other things, that we have finally entered the new age to which Father Bede was referring. A pervasive phenomenon of this new period in human history is the collapse of the boundaries that have separated the religions and cultures for millennia. Part of the reason for this collapse is the rediscovery and recovery of the mystical dimension universally present in all the great world traditions, augmented by the revolution in communications technology. This mystical dimension of experience found in every corner of the globe represents a kind of ultimate common ground that each tradition shares with every other.

Behind the religions as historical institutions is a primary revelation to, or mystical awakening of, their founders. This is the basis of the authenticity of each tradition. In the *Sanatana Dharma*—that is, the Hindu tradition—the inner experience of the *rishis*, the forest sages of ancient India, is the origin of this very deep and rich culture. The mystical awakening, and its subsequent articulation in the Vedas, is the source of Hinduism. Likewise, in the Dharma, or Buddhism, the ground of this profound tradition is the inner process of enlightenment of Gautama Siddhartha Sakyamuni, the Buddha, or Enlightened One. His experience of awakening and enlightenment is paradigmatic for all followers of the Dharma after him. His life and spiritual attainment, which is a mystical process, is a perennial source of inspiration for all generations of Buddhists since the time the Enlightened One walked the earth.

In a similar vein, when we look at the Jewish tradition, we find that Judaism owes its life to the early mystical experience of its patriarchs, prophets, and other biblical figures. Abraham, Isaac, Jacob, Moses, Isaiah, Jeremiah, Ezekiel, Daniel, and countless others are the recipients of a historical revelation from God, Yahweh, and this revelation is a decidedly mystical reality. Revelation is itself a form of mystical experience, though it is inclusive of a whole people, or all of humankind. Revelation in its historical type is a mystical process spanning centuries, even millennia in its unfolding to a community. The biblical revelation is the foundation of the three religions of the Book: Judaism, Christianity, and Islam.

The Christian faith and all the forms of spirituality that derive from it, like the devotional, charismatic, and contemplative, trace their origin and life to the inner awareness of Jesus Christ, who was keenly conscious of an intimate relationship with the Divine, actually with Yahweh, the God of Abraham, Isaac, Jacob, Moses, and the prophets. His inner certitude, his miracles, and his impact on his disciples gave birth to the church. Christianity is now a third of humanity, and in the case of all those who call themselves Christian, Christ is the focus, and his mystical awareness is essential to the identity of anyone in this faith.

Islam is no different from all of the above examples. Its beginnings are found in the private revelation of the Prophet Mohammad in the seventh century. His experience consisted of a verbal revelation of the

Qur'an from Allah, or God, through the mediation of the Archangel Gabriel, presumably the same archangel who appeared to Mary and told her she had been chosen to carry and give birth to God's son, Jesus, the Christ, or the Messiah. Mohammad's encounter with Allah, through Gabriel, lasted some twenty-three years. All of Islam owes its faith to that of the Prophet, and especially his mystical process of hearing the Qur'an and then reciting it.

There is also no doubt that all of the ancient spiritual traditions, like Shintoism; Taoism; the cosmic revelation in the indigenous traditions of Africa, Asia, the Pacific, and the Americas; and the "modern" types found in the West in the Romantic movement, with their towering poets, like Byron, Shelley, Keats, and Wordsworth; the American Transcendentalists, like Emerson, Bronson, Whitman, and Thoreau; and the ecological development, with figures like Matthew Fox, Thomas Berry, and Annie Dillard, are all manifestations of the perennial mystical spirit. In all the above instances, we can see the utter reality, durability, and power of mysticism as the generating source of genuine religion, of authentic faith. The great world religious movements, as we've seen, depend on knowledge of the Divine gained through mystical revelation to bring them into being.

THE END OF MATERIALISM

As the interfaith movement comes of age, as dialogue more and more replaces confrontation, and a new model of community replaces the old one of isolation and antagonism among the faiths—and as scientific knowledge advances, especially in physics, cosmology, mathematics, evolutionary biology, complexity theory, and psychology—materialism, as a paradigm for understanding the world, will be regarded increasingly as untenable. Materialism is a reductionist view that maintains everything is reducible to a material substratum governed by material principles; that the supernatural, the soul, and spiritual experience do not exist; and that consciousness is an epiphenomenon of matter. That view is now being questioned by many scientists, philosophers, and, of course, mystics. Our understanding of matter today does not support the materialist, reductionist view! For instance, quantum physics has discovered that the so-called physical reality is not really made of anything substantial, or anything material. The wave-particle duality is a nonmaterial reality. This is the most basic level of reality, nature, and cosmos, and there is no matter to support it. Rather, what we discover on the level of subatomic particles is that the particles are actually components of information. Materialism literally doesn't have a leg to stand on. There is, thus, in our time, a movement to a science based on the primacy of consciousness that sees all reality arising out of infinite mind.

The new paradigm that is emerging is subtle; it allows for a congenial, mutually respectful relationship between science and religion, or between mysticism and the scientific spirit. They both emanate from the same universal mind; they are part of the system of consciousness itself. In a very real sense, materialism has been holding the human family back by its wholly inadequate view that rejected the spiritual dimension of existence a priori without even looking at the evidence. Many things have called this reductionism into question, chief of which is the reality of mystical experience, the fact that it can be transmitted and awakened in others, that it is in some sense repeatable. Here the Tibetan tradition has been very helpful. The vast experience of people all around the world who have enjoyed the mystical experience testify to the utter truth and reality of mystical consciousness. The stories in this book are evidence of this truth.

INTERSPIRITUALITY AND INTEGRAL SPIRITUALITY

Another significant and permanent feature of the age we have entered is that it can be called an interspiritual and intermystical age. What is meant is a new period in history in which persons of all traditions feel a freedom and an ease to explore the other religions experientially, not primarily in a merely academic sense. They are often finding new elements from other traditions, like methods of prayer and transformation, contemplative and psychological insights, and new ways of expressing or practicing and pursuing their spiritual lives, and are adding them to their previous approach; or they are even setting an old approach aside for a new one.

This development is truly revolutionary, for it takes us beyond the known, the safe, and the secure to the unknown, vulnerable, and changing nature of things. Many of the stories in this book exhibit the spirit of interspirituality. I believe we are in a process of arriving at a new understanding of its necessity for humanity and the earth. Interspirituality, as the progressive core practical consequence of the interfaith movement, is a quantum leap forward toward a unification of the human family. I am not suggesting, however, that interspirituality is a new universal religion—rather that it assumes and uncovers the universal dimension of mystical realization as the essence of religion itself, and therefore of all the authentic traditions themselves.

Interspirituality also strives to be integral in its understanding and articulation. All the religions are included, as they bear the fruit of the mystical life of their great founders. We have the beginning threads of evolution toward an encompassing spirituality that includes art, music (especially in its sacred forms), poetry, literature, philosophy, and film. It includes science and its honest search for the ultimate foundation of reality; it is interested in psychological experience and fascinated with the faculty of imagination, which though often undisciplined is nevertheless a visionary, and hence spiritual, capacity. It also encompasses the unconscious realm of human life and the realm of dream consciousness, where the seeds of attitudes, motivation, behavior, and action have their roots.

Integral spirituality attempts to unite three spheres of existence: the conscious, the unconscious, and the superconscious. It seeks integration of all aspects of both the human and the divine states of being. It desires the whole picture of our experience, not simply culturally determined preferences. It inquires in a practical way as to what actually works to open people up to radical spiritual change or transformation.

This kind of transformation has to be whole or total, as nearly total as is possible in this life.

The integral spiritual approach to transformation illustrated in the stories requires a substantial change in the ways that various aspects of our lives operate. These aspects, all of which are important, include will (intention), character, understanding, memory, imagination, the unconscious, and behavior.

Integral spirituality involves us in a journey to wholeness and refinement of our being. That is essentially what transformation is all about. It has to effect change in every area of our lives, leaving nothing aside. As a person makes progress in the inner journey, there is a wonderful maturing of their character in light of love, compassion, kindness, and mercy toward all beings. Similarly, the understanding of the person is expanded and becomes more subtle, like reality itself. Then the will is engaged in this process of radical alteration of the self, of being freed from compulsions, addictions, fixations, especially that of the false self, the selfish pursuit of oneself. The will commits to the good of others and is centered on their welfare, rather than exclusively on one's own. The memory is healed of its woundedness and is capable of functioning free of trauma and reactions to the past. The imagination works in tandem with all the other faculties in seeking the Divine, not in seeking its own gratification.

Again, the unconscious becomes progressively purified, and the elements of hidden, negative motivation are disengaged, like deleting an unwanted program. Much of the work of the spiritual life concerns this purification of the unconscious. Finally, the changes in all these areas have a profound impact on one's behavior and actions. They become consistent with a higher observance of virtue and holiness, of mercy, compassion, and love. This kind of holistic transformation is characteristic of a mature understanding of spirituality in its integral mode. As our collective understanding across the traditions continues to unfold, the considerations we have outlined here, and many more unstated, will become part of the fabric of our interfaith understanding. Drawing on all traditions in a sort of universal tradition will greatly enrich our view of what mature spirituality is, and will make our own journey more effective, especially as this benefits all those we work to serve.

With this broader understanding, we are already beginning to evolve in the direction of an integral spiritual vision that embraces all areas of knowledge pertaining to living the spiritual journey in our time. We are building the foundation for a viable spirituality that can serve to unite rather than divide humanity for the countless millennia ahead.

CPSIA information can be obtained
at www.ICGtesting.com
Printed in the USA
BVHW030913170520
579804BV00006B/512